# NOMADIC FURNITURE:

HOW TO BUILD AND WHERE TO BUY LIGHTWEIGHT FURNITURE THAT FOLDS, COLLAPSES, STACKS, KNOCKS DOWN, INFLATES OR CAN BE THROWN AWAY AND RECYCLED. BEING BOTH A BOOK OF INSTRUCTION AND A CATALOG of ACCESS FOR EASY MOVING

# NOMADIC FURNITURE:

BY JAMES HENNESSEY & VICTOR PAPANEK WITH MANY EASY~TO~FOLLOW DIAGRAMS, PHOTOGRAPHS AND DRAWINGS BY THE AUTHORS.

PANTHEON BOOKS

A DIVISION OF RANDOM HOUSE, NEW YORK

LIBRARY OF CONGRESS CATALOGING IN PUBLICATION DATA

HENNESSEY, JAMES. NOMADIC FURNITURE.

1. FURNITURE MAKING-AMATEURS' MANUALS.  2. FURNITURE-
CATALOGS.  I. PAPANEK, VICTOR J., JOINT AUTHOR.  II. TITLE.
TT 195.H145  684.1  72-3412
ISBN 0-394-47577-1
ISBN 0-394-70228-X [PBK]

MANUFACTURED IN THE UNITED STATES OF AMERICA

PRINTED AND BOUND BY HALLIDAY LITHOGRAPH
CORPORATION, WEST HANOVER, MASSACHUSETTS

98765432

FIRST EDITION

# table of contents:

Note: throughout this book, all drawings are dimensioned in feet and inches.

# introduction:

_You are nomadic_: AMERICANS ARE SAID TO MOVE ABOUT EVERY 2-3 YEARS ON THE AVERAGE. SOME OF US, LIKE THE WRITERS OF THIS BOOK, MOVE MORE AND MOVE OVER GREATER DISTANCES. VICTOR PAPANEK, FOR INSTANCE, HAS IN THE LAST EIGHTEEN YEARS MOVED FROM LA JOLLA TO SAN FRANCISO, SPENT 5 YEARS IN CANADA, THEN LOCATED IN THE SOUTHERN UNITED STATES, THEN 6 YEARS IN THE MIDWEST, INTERRUPTED BY WORKING AND LIVING FOR MINIMAL PERIODS OF 3-9 MONTHS, IN THE UNITED ARAB REPUBLIC, BALI & JAVA, JAPAN, FINLAND, SWEDEN, AUSTRIA & GERMANY. AT THE TIME OF THIS WRITING, PAPANEK IS PREPARING TO MOVE HIS WIFE, TWO-YEAR-OLD DAUGHTER & HIMSELF TO DENMARK FOR A YEAR. AFTER THAT BECKONS TANZANIA, ZAMBIA, UGANDA.... JIM HENNESSEY HAS TREKKED FROM CHICAGO TO STOCKHOLM, MOVED HIS SMALL SON & WIFE TO SOUTHERN CALIFORNIA & IS NOW CONTEMPLATING ANOTHER MOVE TO EIRE OR SCANDINAVIA.... BUT MORE TYPICALLY: THE ELECTRICAL INSPECTOR LIVING ABOVE US [WITH 3 KIDS] HAS BEEN TRANSFERRED 22 TIMES IN 4 YEARS! OUR DOCTOR HAS LIVED IN SWITZERLAND FOR 2 YEARS, IN AUSTRIA FOR 3, AND IS NOW THINKING OF MOVING TO AUSTRALIA..... THE GARAGE MECHANIC LIVING AT THE CORNER HAS WORKED IN 9 DIFFERENT STATES IN THE U.S., COMES FROM HUNGARY & IS PLANNING TO MOVE

TO NOVA SCOTIA NEXT WEEK.... INDUSTRY & ACADEME, THE MILITARY AND, MOST IMPORTANTLY, CHANGING LIFE-STYLES AMONG YOUNG PEOPLE, TEND TO MAKE US ALL MORE NOMADIC.

The Problem: BASICALLY WE CAN BUY FURNITURE, BUILD IT or INHERIT IT. ALL OF IT IS BULKY, HEAVY, OFTEN FRAGILE & ALWAYS A BITCH TO MOVE. THERE ARE HUNDREDS OF BOOKS TO TELL US "HOW-TO" DESIGN & "BUILD-IT-YOURSELF". ALSO EVEN MORE BOOKS TO TELL US WHAT TO BUY [& WHERE & FOR HOW MUCH!]. OFTEN THERE MAY BE ONE or TWO KNOCK~DOWN OR FOLDING or INFLATABLE PIECES INCLUDED, BUT JUST ACCIDENTALLY.

BUT THERE IS NO BOOK THAT SHOWS HOW TO BUILD FURNITURE THAT IS EASY TO MAKE, BUT FURNITURE WHICH ALSO FOLDS, STACKS, INFLATES OR KNOCKS DOWN or ELSE IS DISPOSABLE WHILE BEING ECOLOGICALLY RE~SPONSIBLE!

NOR IS THERE ANY BOOK THAT SHOWS WHAT EXISTS ON THE MARKET [IN THE U.S. AND ABROAD] THAT MAKES SENSE FOR NOMADIC LIVING.

IT'S NOT A NEW PROBLEM:
THE EGYPTIANS USED A STOOL, AS WELL AS FOLDING BEDS. EGYPTIAN "X" SHAPE LATER ADOPTED BY THE ROMANS, ITS SOFTENED CURVES CARRIED OVER TO THE "SAVONAROLA" FOLDING THRONE OF THE RENAISSANCE.) FOLDING THIS FOLDING WAS ALSO BUT ESSENTIALLY ALL FURNITURE THROUGHOUT HISTORY HAS BEEN A SIGN of OPULENCE & SPLENDOUR, STATIC STATUS SYMBOL OF A

CLASS THAT OWNED LANDS & RARELY MOVED. THIS MEXICAN STOOL of 3 WOODEN RODS, SOME TWINE AND A LEATHER TRIANGLE WITH A POCKET SEWN INTO THE CORNERS ON THE UNDER~SIDE, IS INGENIOUS. BASICALLY IT IS BUCKY FULLER'S "CONTINUOUS~TENSION~DISCONTINUOUS~COMPRESSION" STRUCTURE of 2 OPPOSED & OPEN TETRAHEDRA. THE MORE LOAD APPLIED, THE STRONGER THE SUPPORT BECOMES. (LATELY THIS STOOL HAS BEEN PROMOTED FOR SUNDAY PAINTERS.)

## The Solution:

WE HAVE PUT TOGETHER A CATALOG OF FURNITURE YOU CAN BUILD YOURSELF EASILY, OR BUY OR ADAPT. WE ARE GIVING YOU INSTRUCTIONS ON WHAT TO BUY OR MAKE, AND WHERE. ALL OF IT CAN BE FOLDED OR KNOCKED DOWN, STACKED, INFLATED OR [ECOLOGICALLY RESPONSIBLY] RE~CYCLED OR THROWN AWAY.

## What's wrong with this Book?

NO BOOK LIKE THIS HAS EVER BEEN PUT TOGETHER BEFORE. SO MUCH IS MISSING. SOME OF OUR IDEAS ARE REALLY NEW, SOME FROM CULTURES THAT ARE THOUSANDS OF YEARS OLD, STILL OTHERS COME FROM SUCH EMINENT SOURCES AS "TRUE MECHANICS", "REAL SHOP ILLUSTRATED," AND OTHER SUCH JOURNALS DEVOTED TO MEN ATTEMPTING TO CONVERT LIVING PLYWOOD INTO A PUMP~HANDLE LAMP, OR TO BUILD A BETTER KNICK~KNACK~NOOK. THE REAL VALUE OF THIS BOOK IS THAT IT WILL ENABLE ALL OF US NOMADS TO HAVE MORE BY OWNING LESS.

THIS BOOK IS NEW. AESTHETICALLY IT IS CLOSER TO THE "WHOLE EARTH CATALOG" THAN, SAY "MOBILIA". IDEALLY THESE FIRST, PRAGMATIC, TENTATIVE HINTS WILL HELP YOU TO DO THINGS THAT HAVE A GOOD FIT BETWEEN THE WAY IT WORKS & THE WAYS IN WHICH WE FIND DELIGHT. IF SOME OF OUR FIRST ATTEMPTS SEEM CRUDE, REMEMBER THAT GERTRUDE STEIN QUOTED PICASSO:

"When you make a thing, a thing that is new,
it is so complicated making it
that it is bound to be ugly.
        But those that make it after you,
they don't have to worry about making it.
And they can make it pretty, and so everybody
can like it
when the others make it after you..."

WE DEDICATE THIS BOOK TO ALL NOMADIC CULTURES, THOSE THAT HAVE BECOME SEDENTARY AS WELL AS THOSE THAT WILL TASTE FREEDOM AGAIN.

*James W. Hennessey*

STOCKHOLM ~ VALENCIA
1971 ~ 72

*Victor*

VIENNA ~ VALENCIA ~ KØPENHAVN
1971 ~ 72

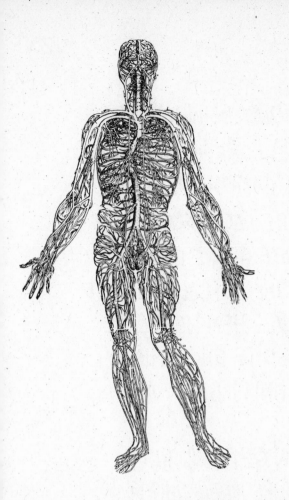

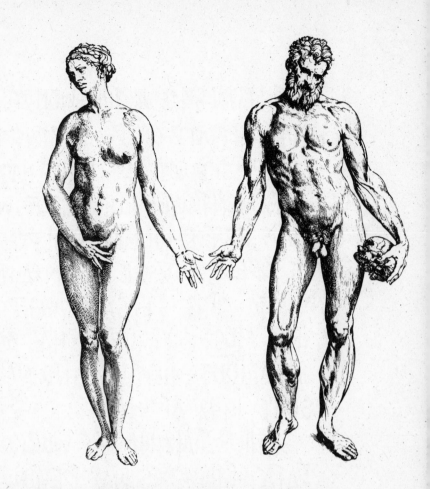

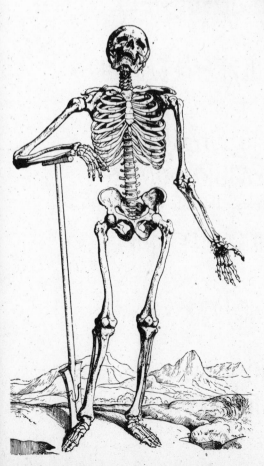

# ON HUMAN MEASUREMENT:

DOZENS OF BOOKS CAN BE, AND I AM AFRAID HAVE BEEN, WRITTEN ABOUT HUMAN SIZE AND OUR ABILITY TO SEE, HEAR, SMELL, REACH, AND PERFORM CERTAIN MUSCULAR TASKS.

IT HAS BECOME SO POPULAR TO MEASURE OURSELVES, THAT IN 25 SHORT YEARS WE HAVE ESCALATED THAT SIMPLE STATISTIC ACTIVITY FROM "HUMAN MEASURE" TO "HUMAN FACTORS", TO "HUMAN ENGINEERING" AND FINALLY CLOAKED THIS FRENETIC BOOK-KEEPING UNDER THE PSEUDO~SCIENTIFIC MANTLE OF "ANTHROPOMETRICS" OR "ERGONOMICS"! ⑤

BUT IN SPITE OF THE WONDERFUL WAY IN WHICH WE HAVE IMPROVED ON DESCRIPTIVE TERMS FOR THIS MEASURING ACTIVITY, THE ACTIVITY ITSELF HAS NOT IMPROVED:

AS MENTIONED ELSEWHERE, WE STILL LACK BASIC SIZE STATISTICS FOR WOMEN, CHILDREN, BABIES, THE ELDERLY, THE OBESE, AND THE INHABITANTS OF THE SO~CALLED "THIRD WORLD." THIS IS EASY TO UNDERSTAND, WHEN WE RECALL THAT <u>MOST</u> MEASURING HAS BEEN DONE ON MEMBERS OF VARIOUS MILITARY AND NAVAL UNITS ONLY, AND SINCE 1942 AT THAT.

WHILE JIM & VIC ARE WORKING ON GETTING SUCH DATA, THIS GOES WAY BEYOND THE SCOPE OF THIS BOOK.

WE HAVE THEREFORE RESTRICTED OURSELVES TO ONLY THOSE BASIC SIZES THAT ARE ABSOLUTELY ESSENTIAL.

WE HAVE SOME COMMENTS ON CHILDREN & BABIES FURTHER ON IN THIS BOOK.

ALSO EVERY PIECE IN THIS BOOK IS SIZED. WE ALSO SUGGEST THAT YOU LITERALLY MEASURE YOUR~ SELF, YOUR WIFE & KIDS. NOTE THESE FINDINGS IN THE BACK PAGES.

IF YOU STILL WANT FURTHER HELP, THERE ARE THREE EXCELLENT BOOKS:

HENRY DREYFUSS: "THE MEASURE OF MAN" [REV.]. NEW YORK: WHITNEY LIBRARY OF DESIGN, 1967.

"DESIGNING FOR PEOPLE". NEW YORK: SIMON AND SCHUSTER, 1951.

PANERO, JULIUS, AND REPETTO, NINO, "ANATOMY FOR INTERIOR DESIGNERS" <u>3</u>RD EDITION, N.Y.: WHITNEY LIBRARY OF DESIGN, 1962.

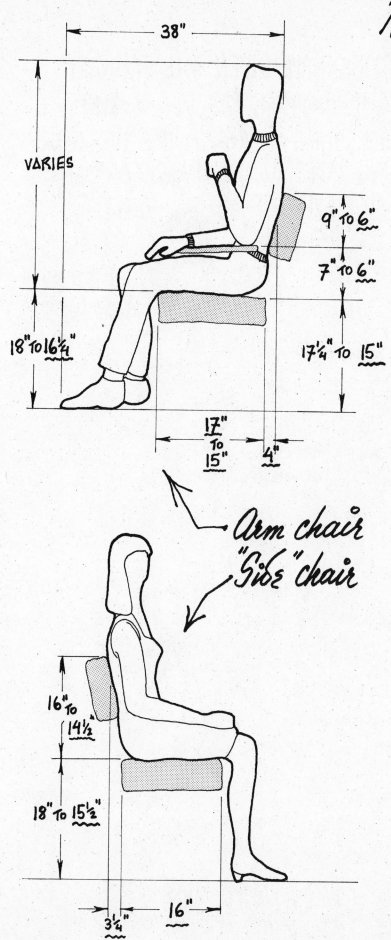

38"

VARIES

9" TO 6"

7" TO 6"

18" TO 16¾"

17¼" TO 15"

17" TO 15"

4"

Arm chair
"Side" chair

16" TO 14½"

18" TO 15½"

3¼"

16"

IN ALL of OUR MEASUREMENTS
WE HAVE TRIED TO GIVE A
RANGE of MEASUREMENTS.
WE HAVE WORKED WITH 16
EUROPEAN & AMERICAN BOOKS.
THE FIRST NUMBER IS ALWAYS
THE "STANDARD" NUMBER,
AND THE ONE YOU'LL BE
STUCK WITH IF YOU BUY
READYMADES.
THE SECOND NUMBER IS
UNDERLINED LIKE THIS,
AND IT IS THE MEASURE
WE FEEL TO BE MOST
COMFORTABLE. VIC IS 5'8½",
JIM 6'1", HARLANNE 5'6" &
SARA HENNESSEY ABOUT 5'9".
NATURALLY WE HAVE EXPERI-
MENTED WITH OTHER
FRIENDS AS WELL.
WE FEEL THAT OUR UNDERLINED
SIZES REFLECT CHANGING
WAYS of SITTING & WORKING.
WE SUGGEST YOU WORK WITHIN
OUR REVISED PARAMETERS.

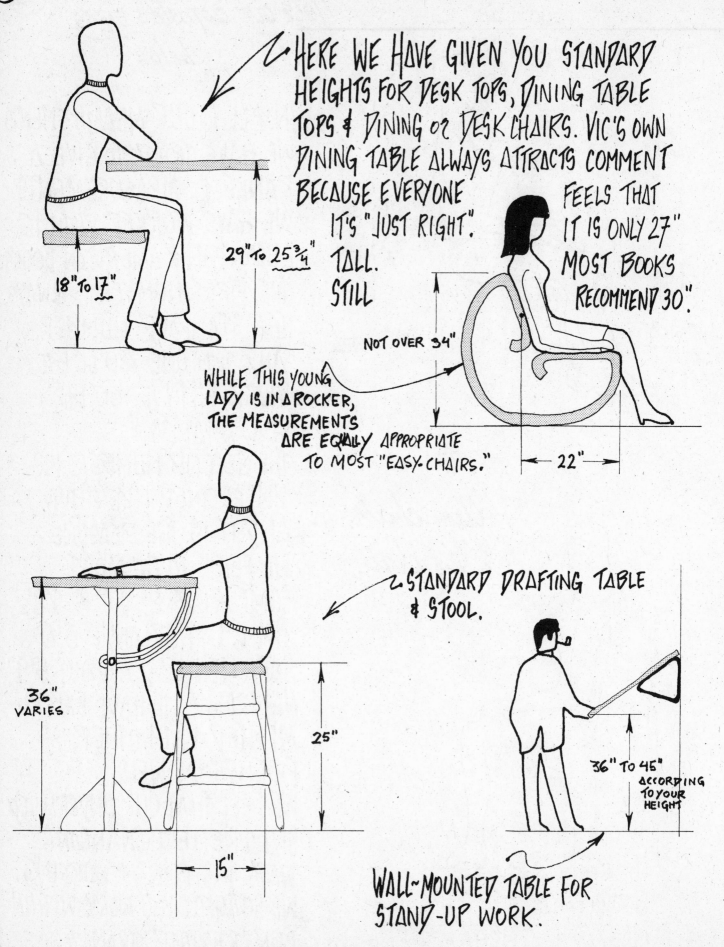

HERE WE HAVE GIVEN YOU STANDARD HEIGHTS FOR DESK TOPS, DINING TABLE TOPS & DINING OR DESK CHAIRS. VIC'S OWN DINING TABLE ALWAYS ATTRACTS COMMENT BECAUSE EVERYONE IT'S "JUST RIGHT". TALL. STILL

FEELS THAT IT IS ONLY 27" MOST BOOKS RECOMMEND 30".

29" TO 25¾"

18" TO 17"

NOT OVER 34"

WHILE THIS YOUNG LADY IS IN A ROCKER, THE MEASUREMENTS ARE EQUALLY APPROPRIATE TO MOST "EASY-CHAIRS."

22"

STANDARD DRAFTING TABLE & STOOL.

36" VARIES

25"

15"

36" TO 45" ACCORDING TO YOUR HEIGHT

WALL~MOUNTED TABLE FOR STAND-UP WORK.

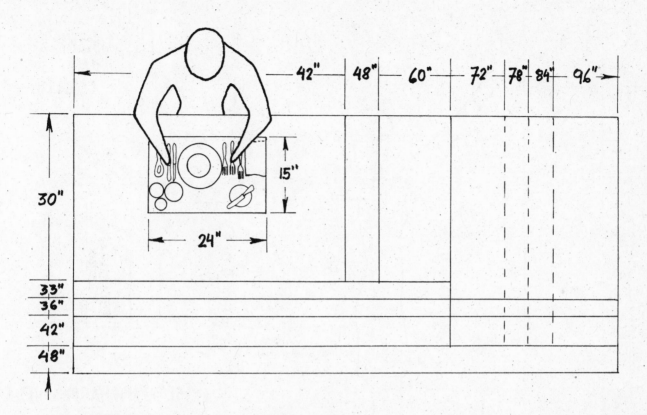

RECTANGULAR TABLE SIZES ARE GIVEN ABOVE. THE MAT IS AN UNUSUALLY LARGE ONE, STANDARD ONES ARE OFTEN AS SKIMPY AS 12"×18". FOR COMFORTABLE SEATING ALLOW 26" PER PERSON, MINIMALLY 22". IF PEOPLE ARE ALSO TO SIT AT THE NARROW ENDS, TABLES SHOULD BE MINIMALLY 34" WIDE.

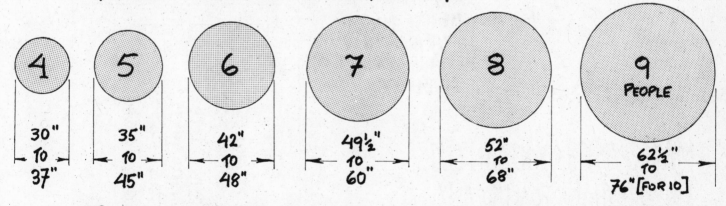

| 4 | 5 | 6 | 7 | 8 | 9 PEOPLE |
|---|---|---|---|---|---|
| 30" TO 37" | 35" TO 45" | 42" TO 48" | 49½" TO 60" | 52" TO 68" | 62½" TO 76" [FOR 10] |

ROUND TABLES ARE VERY DIFFICULT TO COMPUTE: THE SMALLER FIGURE IN EACH CASE ABOVE IS FOR VERY SNUG SEATING, THE LARGER FIGURE FOR COMFORT. WE HAVE INCLUDED THESE BECAUSE VIC SAW MANY ROUND TABLES WHEN TRAVELLING TO COMMUNES.

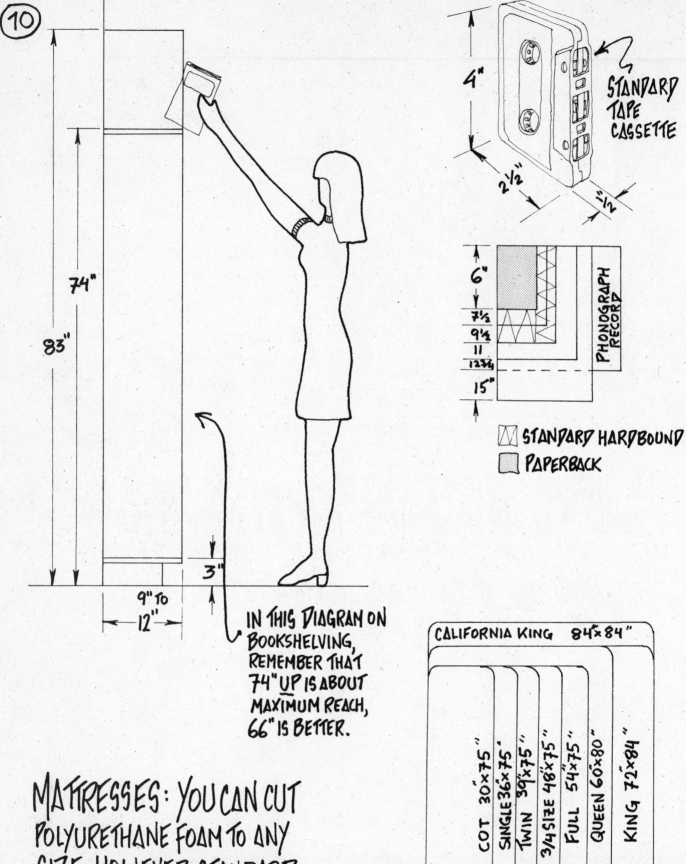

74"

83"

3"

9" TO 12"

STANDARD TAPE CASSETTE

4"

2½"

½"

6"

7½"

9½"

11

12¾

15"

PHONOGRAPH RECORD

STANDARD HARDBOUND

PAPERBACK

IN THIS DIAGRAM ON BOOKSHELVING, REMEMBER THAT 74" UP IS ABOUT MAXIMUM REACH, 66" IS BETTER.

CALIFORNIA KING   84"x 84"

COT 30"x75"
SINGLE 36"x75"
TWIN 39"x75"
¾ SIZE 48"x75"
FULL 54"x75"
QUEEN 60"x80"
KING 72"x84"

MATTRESSES: YOU CAN CUT POLYURETHANE FOAM TO ANY SIZE. HOWEVER, STANDARD MATTRESS SIZES ARE GIVEN HERE. THICKNESS IN FOAM CAN BE 1", 2", 3", 4", 6".

# SEATING:

PART OF THE PRICE WE PAY FOR WALKING ERECT IS THAT WE MUST SIT DOWN OR LIE DOWN TO RELAX OR WORK AT PRECISE THINGS.

DESIGNERS HAVE TURNED THIS NEARLY UNIVERSAL HUMAN NEED INTO A SERIES OF EGO~TRIPS. THUS CHAIRS HAVE BEEN CALLED: "THE SIGNATURE PIECE OF THE DESIGNER." AT LAST LOOK, OVER 150 BOOKS EXIST THAT DEAL WITH CHAIRS.

SEATING CAN BE DIVIDED INTO THOSE CHAIRS THAT MAKE SENSE FOR EATING & WORKING AT A TABLE OR DESK, THOSE THAT ARE GOOD FOR RELAXING & LOUNGING, THOSE THAT COMBINE BOTH OF THESE FUNCTIONS, SPECIAL-IZED CHAIRS, AND SEATING THAT ACCOMMODATES MORE THAN ONE PERSON ["LOVE~SEATS", "SOFAS," etc.].

MOST SEATING [IF COMFORTABLE] IS BULKY, HEAVY, HARD~TO~MOVE.

WE THINK THAT "DINING" CHAIRS, WHICH ALSO WORK AS DESK CHAIRS, CAN BE BOUGHT CHEAPLY ENOUGH [$3.- TO $6.—] SO THAT YOU SHOULD NOT TRY TO BUILD ONE. BUY WHAT YOU NEED AT THE SALVATION ARMY OR GOODWILL & FINISH THEM NATURALLY, OR PAINT THEM, AND/OR ADD SOME BRIGHT CUSHIONS. ➔ WHEN READY TO MOVE, RECYCLE THEM BACK TO GOODWILL OR TO FRIENDS.

ANOTHER STRATEGY IS TO BUY FOLDING CHAIRS. VIC HAS EIGHT DIRECTORS CHAIRS IN HIS LIVING

ROOM, FOR RELAXING, LOUNGING, ENTERTAINING. BUT THEY DO DOUBLE DUTY: THEY CAN ALSO BE USED AS DINING CHAIRS WHEN MOVED TO THE TABLE.

> note: dining tables if used with directors chairs or other double-duty chairs, must be <u>extra low</u>, see: TABLES.

MOST PURE LOUNGING CHAIRS ARE DIFFERENT IN THAT YOU CAN BUILD THEM YOURSELF: BEANBAGS, FIBRE-BARREL CHAIRS, "TUBE" SOFAS, CORRUGATED CARDBOARD CHAIRS, SIMPLE CHIPBOARD CHAIRS THAT CAN BE UPHOLSTERED. IN THE FOLLOWING PAGES YOU'LL ALSO FIND LOUNGE CHAIRS STRAPPED INTO SHAPE OUT OF OLD MATRESSES.

> When you are really ready to move, please recycle these chairs, don't just pitch them!

ASSUMING YOU'VE JUST FINISHED YOUR GEODESIC DOME, WHAT WILL YOU SIT ON?

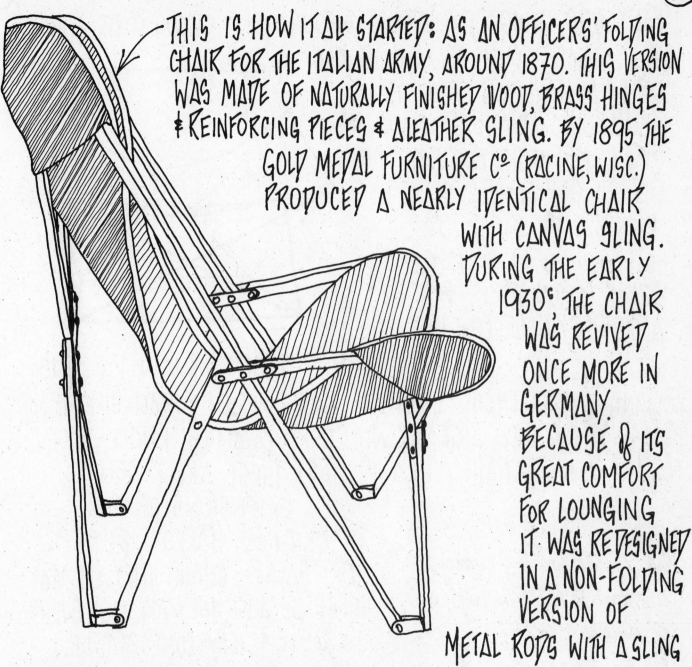

THIS IS HOW IT ALL STARTED: AS AN OFFICERS' FOLDING CHAIR FOR THE ITALIAN ARMY, AROUND 1870. THIS VERSION WAS MADE OF NATURALLY FINISHED WOOD, BRASS HINGES & REINFORCING PIECES & A LEATHER SLING. BY 1895 THE GOLD MEDAL FURNITURE Cº (RACINE, WISC.) PRODUCED A NEARLY IDENTICAL CHAIR WITH CANVAS SLING. DURING THE EARLY 1930s, THE CHAIR WAS REVIVED ONCE MORE IN GERMANY. BECAUSE OF ITS GREAT COMFORT FOR LOUNGING IT WAS REDESIGNED IN A NON-FOLDING VERSION OF METAL RODS WITH A SLING

OF LEATHER OR LINEN, BY ANTONIO BONET, JUAN KURCHAN & JORGE FERRARI-HARDOY IN 1938. IT IMMEDIATELY BECAME AN EXPENSIVE & "TRENDY" INDOOR/OUTDOOR CHAIR, MARKETED BY KNOLL INTERNATIONAL. SINCE THEN ITS PRICE HAS DROPPED TO LESS THAN $10—. THE METAL PARTS OF SEVERAL OF THESE CHAIRS STACK AND YOU CAN MAKE

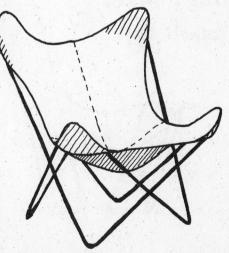

FANTASTIC SLINGS BY SORTING THROUGH OLD RACOON COATS, FURS, YOUR GREAT-UNCLE'S POLAR BEAR RUG, OR WHAT-HAVE-YOU FROM THE SALVATION ARMY STORE OR A SWAP MEET. → SEW THE FUR RIGHT ON THE OLD CANVAS SLING. → OR USE BRIGHT PRINTS (marimekko?) → OR TIE~DYE HEAVY COTTON DUCK. → OR GET A SHEEP~SKIN OR COW~HIDE.

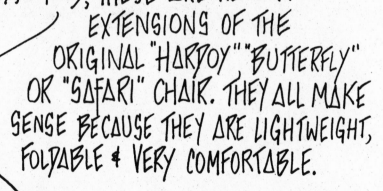

IN 1964 PIERRE PAULIN DID THIS FOLDING GARDEN CHAIR (IN "CHROME~PLATED METAL & BUFFALO HIDE" IF YOU PLEASE!) IN FRANCE. TOGETHER WITH ESKO PAJAMIES' KNOCK~DOWN METAL & CANVAS CHAIR (FINLAND, 1965), THESE ARE RECENT EXTENSIONS OF THE ORIGINAL "HARDOY" "BUTTERFLY" OR "SAFARI" CHAIR. THEY ALL MAKE SENSE BECAUSE THEY ARE LIGHTWEIGHT, FOLDABLE & VERY COMFORTABLE.

Note: Metal folding chairs are hard to build because of hinges & welding. So buy these if you can, otherwise, turn the page!

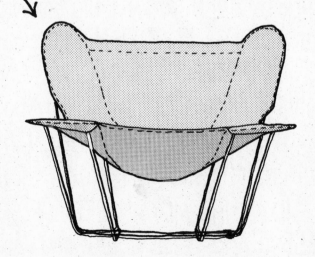

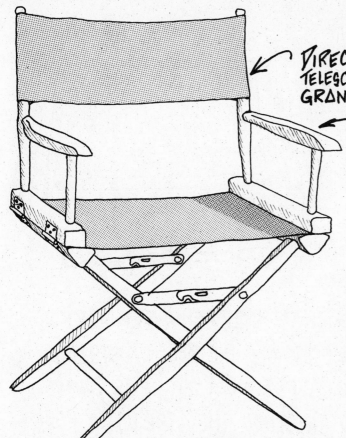

DIRECTORS CHAIR, CURRENTLY MADE BY THE TELESCOPE FOLDING FURNITURE Co. INC. of GRANVILLE, N.Y., U.S.A.

THIS IS AN OLD STAND-BY: VERY COMFORTABLE FOR WRITING, DINING OR LOUNGING. YOU CAN BUY IT FROM SEARS, ROEBUCK & Co., OR ANY OUTDOOR FURNITURE STORE. NEW IT COSTS BETWEEN $9.– & $15.–. IT FOLDS, & SEAT & BACK ARE N°8 DUCK. HERE AGAIN YOU CAN COVER IT WITH PIECES OF FUR [SEWN TO THE CANVAS], OR WITH BRIGHT COTTON OR LEATHER. YOU CAN EVEN *WEAVE* A BACK & SEAT FOR IT AS HARLANNE PAPANEK HAS DONE. (BELOW)

VERSIONS OF THIS CHAIR ARE MADE ALL OVER THE WORLD. "STATUS" INTERPRETATIONS EXIST IN CHROMED STEEL & SNOW LEOPARD HIDE!

NATURALLY THERE ARE MANY OTHER CHAIRS THAT COMBINE INGENIOUS SYSTEMS FOR A FOLDING LOUNGE SEAT. ONE OF THE MOST INNOVATIVE FROM A STRUCTURAL VIEW

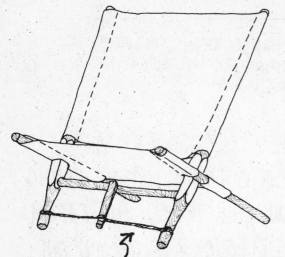

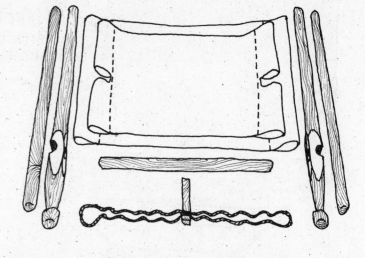

IS THIS COLLAPSIBLE CHAIR OF
BEECHWOOD AND CANVAS BY OLE GJERLØV~KNUDSEN of DENMARK.
THE CANVAS CAN BE LOOSENED & SLIPPED OFF THE BEECH POSTS. THE
WHOLE UNIT THEN COMES APART & CAN BE WRAPPED IN ITS OWN
CANVAS. TENSION IS ADJUSTED BY TWISTING THE STRETCHER ROPE
THAT SPANS THE TWO FRONT LEGS. THIS IS THE SAME METHOD USED
ON AN ORDINARY BUCK~SAW. IT CAN BE ORDERED FROM "DEN
PERMANENTE" IN COPENHAGEN, DENMARK ←

A SIMILAR LOUNGING
POSITION EXISTS IN THIS LIGHT~
WEIGHT FOLDING CHAIR OF STEEL
TUBING & LINEN or CANVAS. IT
WAS DESIGNED BY LINDAU &
LINDECRANTZ & IS AVAILABLE
FROM:

LAMMHULTS MEKANISKA VERKSTAD AB,
S-360 30 LAMMHULT, SWEDEN. ←

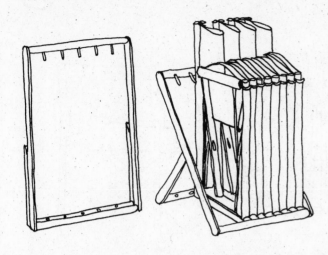

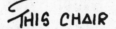

THIS CHAIR

BY MOGENS KOCH of DENMARK WAS
DESIGNED NEARLY 40 YEARS AGO. IT IS, HOWEVER,
STILL ONE OF THE MOST POPULAR FURNITURE PIECES WHICH DENMARK
EXPORTS. IT IS A FOLDING CHAIR, AVAILABLE IN BEECHWOOD & LINEN
CANVAS, OR FOR THE STATUS CROWD, IN ROSEWOOD & LEATHER. ALL
HARDWARE FITTINGS ARE SOLID BRASS. ESPECIALLY IN NORDIC EUROPE
IT FILLS THE PLACE OF THE DIRECTORS CHAIR. AS SHOWN TO THE LEFT
(ABOVE) SIX OF THE CHAIRS, WHEN FOLDED, FIT INTO A SPECIALLY DESIGNED
STORAGE RACK [WHICH ALSO FOLDS]. THE
GREAT VALUE of THIS CHAIR [LIKE THE
DIRECTORS CHAIR] IS THAT IT WORKS EQUALLY
WELL FOR DINING, DESK WORK or LOUNGING,
INDOORS or OUTDOORS. → AVAILABLE from
"INTERNA", COPENHAGEN, DENMARK.

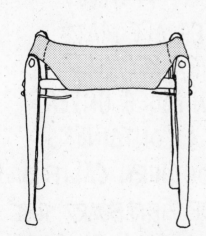

← BEECHWOOD & LINEN FOLDING STOOL BY
AXEL THYGESEN, DENMARK. → ALSO
AVAILABLE FROM "INTERNA".

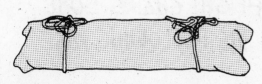

STILL ANOTHER VERSION OF THE DANISH DIRECTORS CHAIR, THIS ONE IS ——→ MADE OF CHROME=STEEL TUBING & CANVAS.

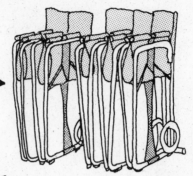

DESIGNED BY LINDAU AND LINDEKRANTZ. AS YOU CAN SEE, THESE ALSO FOLD & STORE IN THEIR OWN RACK. → AVAILABLE FROM: LAMMHULTS MEKANISKA VERKSTAD AB, S-360 30 LAMMHULT, SWEDEN. THEY COST ABOUT $20⁰⁰ ea. AND ARE CALLED: "REGISSÖRSSTOL S-70".

## Fibre Barrels & Fibre Tubs, Tubes & Such:

CHEMICALS, PLASTIC PELLETS & MUCH ELSE ARE SHIPPED IN CARDBOARD OR FIBREBOARD BARRELS. THE FIBREBOARD ITSELF IS USUALLY MADE OF RECYCLED MATERIALS. HARDBOARD DRUMS & TUBES ARE MADE OF BY-PRODUCTS OF THE LUMBER INDUSTRY, RECYCLED RAGS & PAPER. → LOOK IN YOUR YELLOW PAGES UNDER FIBREBOARD PRODUCTS, HARDBOARD & CONTAINERS.

JIM & PENNY HULL, 2 SOUTHERN CALIFORNIA DESIGNERS, HAVE DEVELOPED A SERIES OF FIBREBOARD TUBE CHAIRS, SOFAS, LOVESEATS & WORKING-HEIGHT CHAIRS. SOME OF THEIR CONCEPTS ARE SHOWN ON THE FOLLOWING PAGE OR TWO.

# Cardboard, Corrugated & Double~Corrugated Boards:

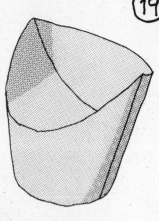

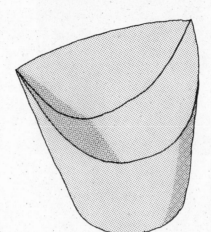

CHILD'S OR ADULT'S SEAT, MADE OF PLASTIC-SURFACED BOARD. DESIGNED & MADE BY PETER MURDOCH, N.Y.

DURING THE EARLY AND MID~SIXTIES, A WHOLE SERIES OF PLASTIC-COATED or FIBREBOARD CHAIRS, OF WHICH THIS IS A GOOD EXAMPLE, BEGAN TO APPEAR ON THE MARKET. AIMED LARGELY AT THE CHILDREN'S, SUB~TEEN & STUDENT CONSTITUENCIES, THE CHAIRS WERE MADE OF PRE~SCORED PATTERNS WITH BRIGHT COLOURS SILK~SCREENED ON. BUYERS WOULD FOLD THEM ALONG THE PRE~SCORED LINES. NO CUTTING WAS REQUIRED, SINCE THE CHAIR PATTERNS WERE DIE~CUT. A SIMPLE BRASS RIVET or STRING~TIE CLOSURE WOULD COMPLETE THE BUILDING PROCESS.

WE ARE NOT SHOWING PRETTY PICTURES OF CARDBOARD CHAIRS YOU CAN BUY IN THIS BOOK. THAT WOULD BE SILLY. EVERYWHERE YOU LOOK THERE IS FREE CORRUGATED. AT SUPERMARKETS & DRUGSTORES YOU CAN GET BOXES. → FOR LARGER PIECES GET APPLIANCE CARTONS. [REFRIGERATORS, WASHERS & DRIERS, etc.]. → SOME BOXES ARE EXTRA HEAVY: LIQUOR, BEER & WINE BOXES, SHIPPING BOXES FOR BANANAS, EGGS, ETC. → SAVE THESE FOR BOOKCASES & "MOVING DAY"!

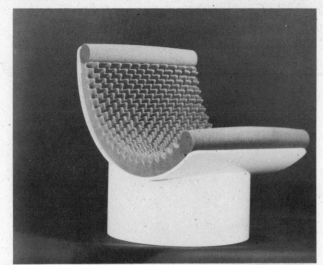

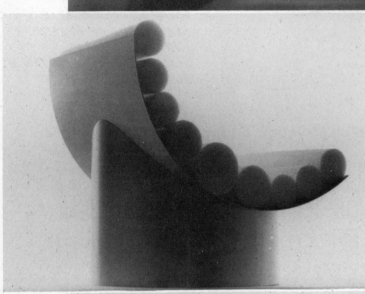

JIM & PENNY HULL ARE BOTH DESIGNERS CONCERNED WITH INTELLIGENT RECYCLING OF MATERIALS.

THE MAJOR STRUCTURAL COMPONENT IN THEIR MANY PIECES OF FURNITURE IS FORMED FIBRE HARDBOARD [WHICH IS IN ITSELF MADE UP OF FIBRE BY-PRODUCTS OF THE LUMBER INDUSTRY, AS WELL AS RECONSTITUTED NEWSPAPERS AND CARDBOARD BOXES].

SINCE GREAT RESEARCH HAS GONE INTO DEVELOPING THESE MATERIALS FOR THE BUILDING INDUSTRY, THE HULLS ARE REALLY RE~ CYCLING BOTH MATERIAL & DEVELOPMENT COSTS.

WE ARE SHOWING A FEW OF THEIR CHAIRS, UPHOLSTERED IN POLYURETHANE FOAM, AS WELL AS A TWO~SEAT COUCH. THE TOP-MOST CHAIR IS UPHOLSTERED IN "FINGER~

FOAM" [CONVOLUTE TEETH OF POLYURETHANE FOAM USED FOR PACKING];
(SEE ALSO DOUGLAS SCHOEFFLER'S LOUNGE ON PAGE 33).

THE MOST RECENT OF THEIR CREATIONS IS "TOOBS",
PICTURED BELOW, A CHILD'S PLAY AND SLEEP ENVIRONMENT.

ONE OF THE MOST EXCITING CONCEPTS OF THE HULLS'
LINE, IS THE IDEA THAT FURNITURE
SHOULD BE AVAILABLE IN VARIOUS
STAGES OF COMPLETION. THUS
IT IS POSSIBLE TO BUY JUST THE
CHAIR BASE, OR THE CHAIR UN-
PAINTED, OR PAINTED OR COVERED
WITH CHROME MYLAR. EQUALLY
WIDE IS THE CHOICE OF UPHOLSTERY:
FLAT CUSHIONS, CYLINDER CUSHIONS
OR "FINGER-FOAM." NATURALLY THERE
ARE VAST PRICE DIFFERENCES.

FINALLY THE HULLS, THROUGH THEIR FIRM CALLED "H.U.D.D.L.E."
WILL ALSO SELL PLAIN TUBES IN DIAMETERS OF
10", 13", 17½", 24," AND 36," AND IN LENGTHS UP TO 80",
BY THE FOOT. THERE IS A MINIMAL CUTTING
CHARGE FOR THIS.

→ JIM & PENNY HULL, H.U.D.D.L.E.
10918 KINROSS AVENUE, WESTWOOD,
LOS ANGELES, CALIF. 90024

h.u.d.d.l.e. environments 10918 kinross. westwood.la.ca. 90024 478-1112

FRANK O. GEHRY, A YOUNG ARCHITECT IN SOUTHERN CALIFORNIA, HAS DEVELOPED A NEW MATERIAL BY LAMINATING LAYERS OF CORRUGATED FIBREBOARD. HE CALLS THE MATERIAL "EDGEBOARD". SHOWN HERE IS HIS MOST MATURELY DEVELOPED DESIGN, A SPRINGY ROCKING CHAIR. IT RETAILS FOR ABOUT $70⁰⁰.

"EDGEBOARD" HAS A TACTILE QUALITY THAT IS SIMILAR TO VELVET, BUT IS STRONGER THAN HARDWOOD, [3 BAR STOOLS WILL SUPPORT A STANDARD VW AUTOMOBILE].

AS A MATERIAL, "EDGE~ BOARD" IS NEARLY IM~ PERVIOUS TO DENTING, MARRING OR SCRATCHING. EVEN CHAR MARKS FROM A CIGARETTE CAN BE

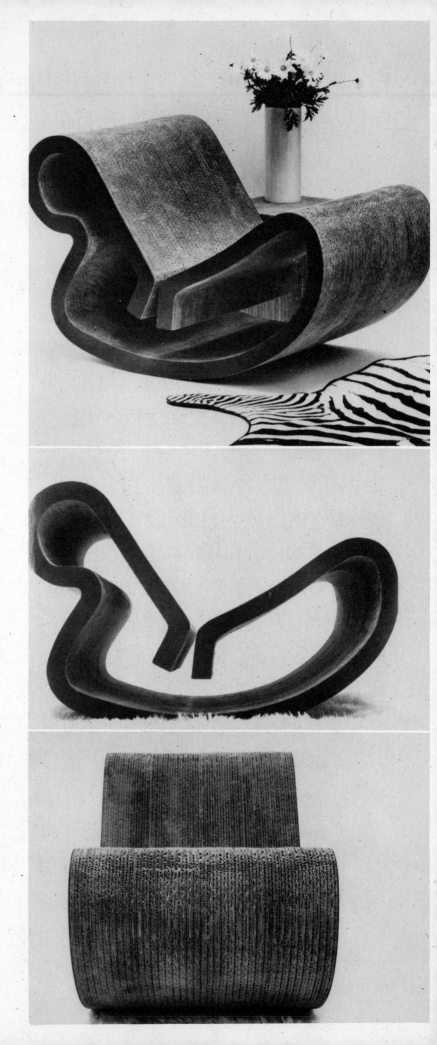

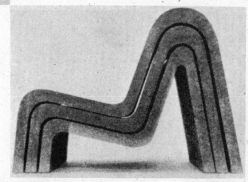

REMOVED WITH A STEEL SUEDE BRUSH, OR SANDPAPER. SPRAY WAX PROTECTS THE SURFACES, SO THAT SPILLED LIQUIDS CAN BE MOMENTARILY SPONGED AWAY.

MOST INTERESTINGLY, THE MATERIAL HAS SOME UNUSUAL SOUND~ABSORBING PROPERTIES, SO THAT IT WILL REDUCE NOISE AT ITS SOURCE BY AS MUCH AS 50 PER-CENT.

WHILE GEHRY'S LINE INCLUDES DINING TABLES, DESKS, COMPONENTS FOR BOOKCASES, BAR STOOLS & MUCH ELSE, ALL OF IT AT A LOW PRICE, WE HAVE ONLY SHOWN HIS THREE NESTING CHAIRS [ABOVE] WHICH WILL SELL FOR LESS THAN $90.00 PER SET.

→ AVAILABLE FROM: "EASY EDGES" INC.
1524 CLOVERFIELD BLVD.
SANTA MONICA, CALIFORNIA, U.S.A.

→ THINK ABOUT WHAT YOU MIGHT DEVELOP FROM LAMINATES!

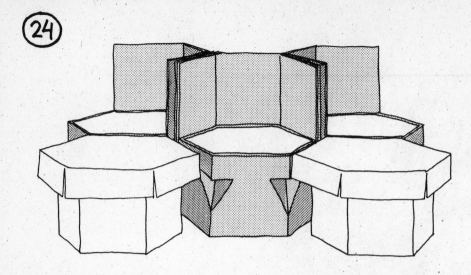

↖ IN THE MID-SIXTIES, PETER RAACKE DEVELOPED THESE HEXAGONAL SEATING UNITS IN GERMANY. THEY ARE QUITE UNCOMFORTABLE. NONETHELESS WE ARE SHOWING THEM HERE, BECAUSE HEXAGONS ARE AN INTELLIGENT WAY OF "CLOSE~PACKING" SPACE. SO TRY YOUR OWN (& HOPEFULLY COLOURFUL) VARIATIONS OF THE ABOVE.

FOR THIS BOOK, VIC SPECIFICALLY INVENTED THE SIMPLEST POSSIBLE CHAIR THAT COULD BE MADE OF SINGLE~CORRUGATED CARDBOARD, WITHOUT ANY RIVETS, GLUE, FASTENERS OR EVEN TABS. ↘

IT MAY NOT BE THE MOST COMFORTABLE CHAIR IN THIS BOOK, BUT IT IS THE MOST "ELEGANT" IN TERMS OF MATERIAL USE. MOST IMPORTANT → IT IS DINING OR DESK~WORK HEIGHT. NATURALLY IT FOLDS ABSOLUTELY FLAT. HOW TO MAKE IT IS SHOWN ON THE NEXT PAGE.

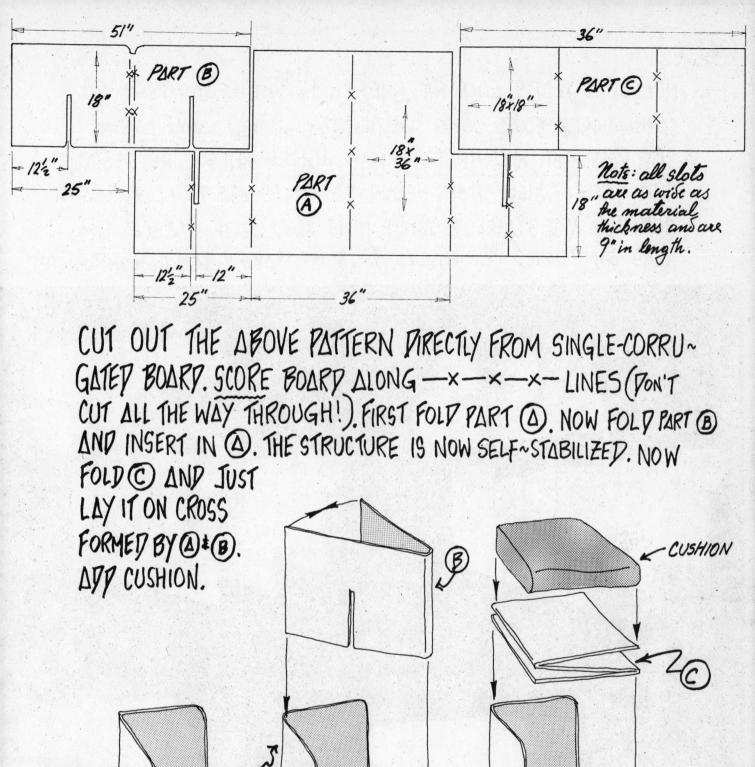

CUT OUT THE ABOVE PATTERN DIRECTLY FROM SINGLE~CORRU~ GATED BOARD. SCORE BOARD ALONG —x—x—x— LINES (DON'T CUT ALL THE WAY THROUGH!). FIRST FOLD PART Ⓐ. NOW FOLD PART Ⓑ AND INSERT IN Ⓐ. THE STRUCTURE IS NOW SELF~STABILIZED. NOW FOLD Ⓒ AND JUST LAY IT ON CROSS FORMED BY Ⓐ & Ⓑ. ADD CUSHION.

Note: all slots are as wide as the material thickness and are 9" in length.

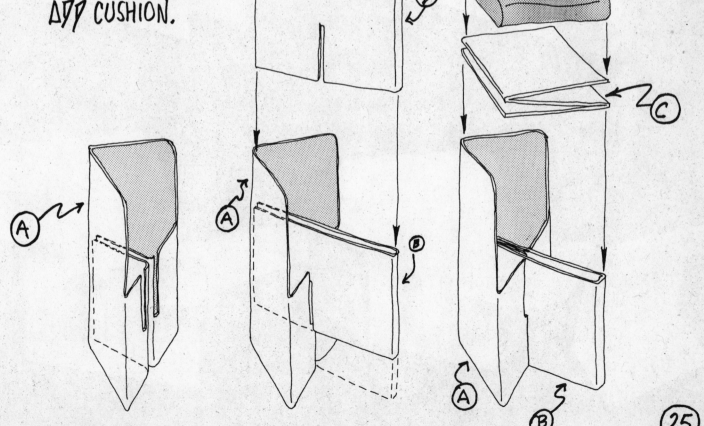

NEARLY 5 YEARS AGO THE SWEDISH FURNITURE COMPANY "DUX" COMMISSIONED FOUR YOUNG SWEDISH DESIGNERS: JANNE AHLIN, JAN DRANGER, MARTIN EISERMAN, JOHAN HULDT. THEY DESIGNED THIS CORRUGATED CHAIR BELOW. THE HOLES ARE FOR CARDBOARD TUBES, TO ADD STABILITY. SINCE IT IS VERY COMFORTABLE, JIM HAS SIMPLIFIED IT. → NEXT PAGE. → MAKE of DOUBLE-CORRUGATED.

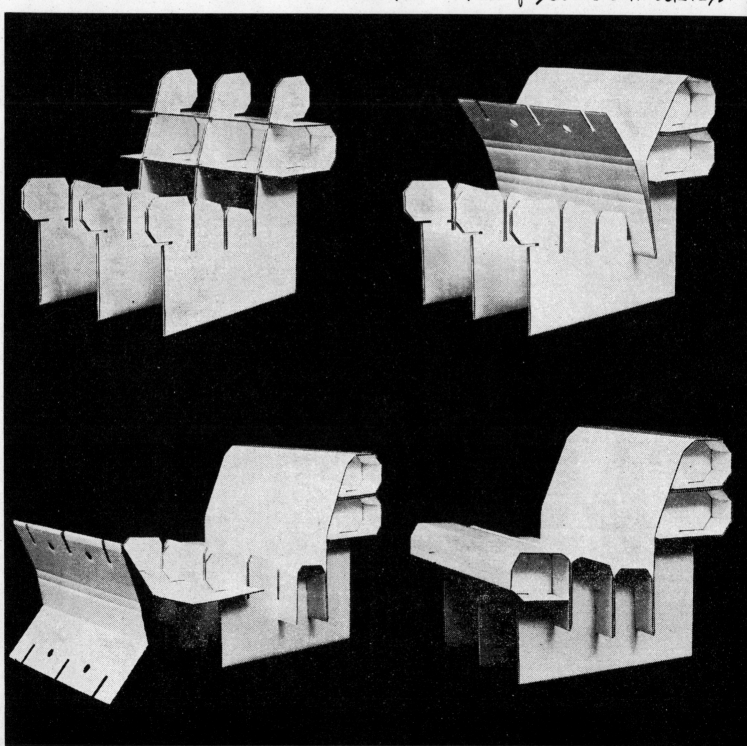

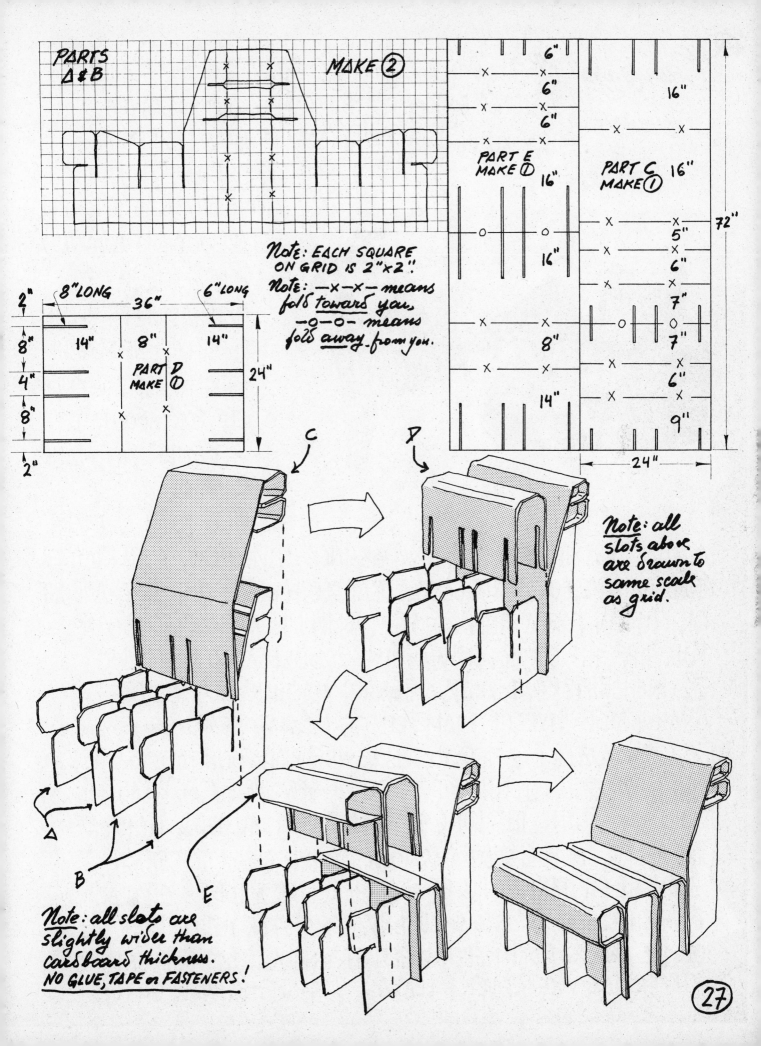

PARTS A & B    MAKE ②

PART E MAKE ①

PART C MAKE ①

6"
6"
6"
16"
16"

16"
16"

8"
14"

72"

16"
5"
6"
7"
7"
6"
9"

24"

Note: EACH SQUARE ON GRID IS 2"×2".

Note: —x—x— means fold toward you, —o—o— means fold away from you.

8" LONG    36    6" LONG

2"
8"
4"
8"
2"

14"    8"    14"

PART D MAKE ①

24"

Note: all slots above are drawn to same scale as grid.

C    D

A    B    E

Note: all slots are slightly wider than cardboard thickness.
NO GLUE, TAPE or FASTENERS!

27

*Bean Bags* ↙ ARE ALL EVOLVED FROM THE "SACCO" (*THE SACK*) CHAIR, DESIGNED BY PIERO GATTI, CESARE PAOLINI & FRANCO TEODORO IN 1968. ORIGINALLY IT WAS A LEATHER SACK (ZIPPERLESS!) & FILLED WITH TINY PLASTIC PELLETS. ALTHOUGH IT ORIGINALLY SOLD FOR NEARLY $90 — MANUFACTURERS BEGAN TO RIP OFF THE DESIGN & SOON PLASTIC VERSIONS SOLD FOR ABOUT $12.50. → BETTER YET, MAKE YOUR OWN! WHAT YOU'LL NEED IS

A LITTLE LESS THAN 6 YARDS of 45-INCH-WIDE HEAVY MATERIAL (NAUGHAHYDE, CORDUROY, CANVAS, SAILCLOTH, etc.) & THE SAME AMOUNT OF MUSLIN FOR A LINER. THAT MUSLIN LINER ENABLES YOU TO PULL OFF THE COVER FOR WASHING. YOU'LL ALSO NEED TWO 22-INCH ZIPPERS, THREAD, A SEWING MACHINE & 15 POUNDS OF GRANULATED STYRENE FOAM PELLETS [*look in yellow pages under:* PLASTICS — FOAM]. AFTER YOU'VE TRANSFERRED OUR PATTERN TO THE MATERIAL, CUT THE PIECES OUT & SEW THE SIX SIDE PANELS TOGETHER ALONG THE LONG SIDES [A-B, C-D]. ALLOW ½ INCH FOR THE SEAM & LAP BOTH SEAM ALLOWANCES TO ONE SIDE & TOP STITCH. SOON ALL SIX PANELS WILL BE TOGETHER, LIKE A TUBE & OPEN AT BOTH ENDS. SEW TOP INTO SMALL END. SEW ZIPPER INTO CENTER SEAM OF THE TWO BOTTOM PIECES & SEW STRONGLY ACROSS BOTH ENDS OF ZIPPER TAPE TO PREVENT LEAKAGE OF STUFFING. NOW STITCH

THE BOTTOM IN THE LARGE END OF THE TUBE TO FORM THE BASE. MAKE THE MUSLIN LINING THE SAME WAY, BUT USE A ⅝-INCH SEAM FOR AN EASIER FIT. NOW SLIP MUSLIN CASING INSIDE OUTER [FABRIC] BAG & ROLL BACK BOTH TOPS FOR FILLING. SINCE THE LIGHTWEIGHT STYRENE FOAM PELLETS ARE STATICALLY CHARGED, USE A LARGE FUNNEL OF HEAVY BROWN PAPER TO FILL THE BAG ABOUT ⅔ FULL. ZIP UP & RELAX!

each square equals 3" →

9"  18"

A  C  TOP MAKE ②  9"

36"

51"

SIDE MAKE ⑥

BOTTOM MAKE ②

21"

15"

B  D  21"

21"

45"

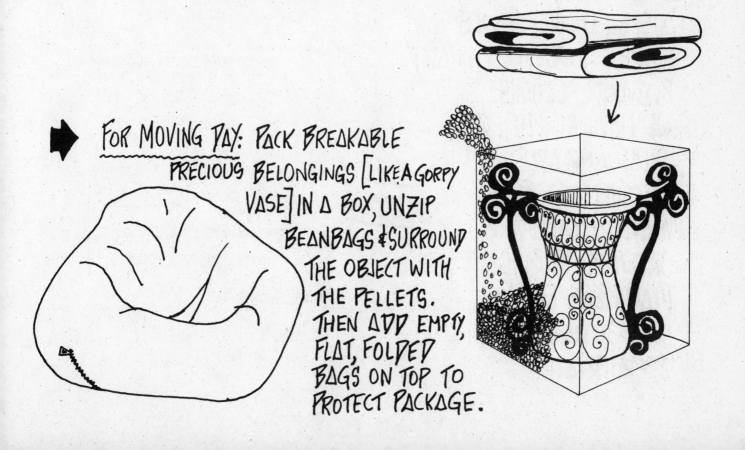

► FOR MOVING DAY: PACK BREAKABLE PRECIOUS BELONGINGS [LIKE A GORPY VASE] IN A BOX, UNZIP BEANBAGS & SURROUND THE OBJECT WITH THE PELLETS. THEN ADD EMPTY, FLAT, FOLDED BAGS ON TOP TO PROTECT PACKAGE.

HERE ARE SOME OTHER IDEAS FOR FIBRE-TUBS:

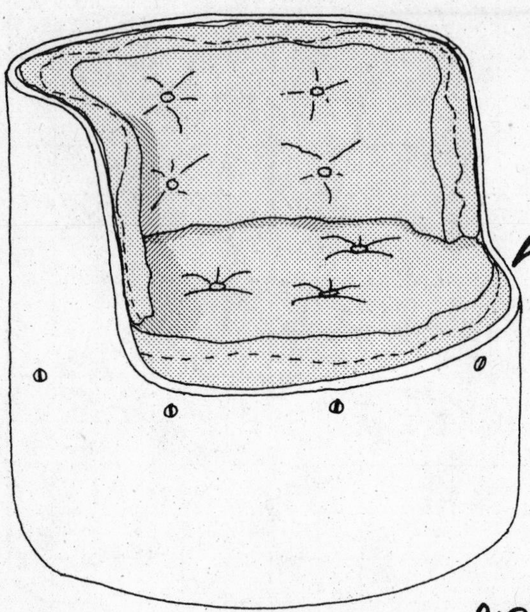

THIS CHAIR SHOULD BE MADE ONLY FROM BARRELS WITH A DIAMETER OF AT LEAST 20 INCHES. THE EXTERIOR OF THE BARREL CAN BE LEFT PLAIN, OR PAINTED. THE SEAT-CUSHION RESTS ON A CIRCLE of WOOD or CHIP-BOARD, GLUED IN OR ATTACHED FROM THE OUTSIDE WITH 2" WOODSCREWS [see below].

IN 1968 WERNER MAERZ, OF GERMANY, DESIGNED A SET of CHAIRS & STOOLS MADE of TUBULAR LAMINATED PLYWOOD SECTIONS. WE HAVE SIMPLIFIED THESE AND ADAPT~ ED THEM TO BE MADE OF CARDBOARD OR FIBRE TUBING. DIAMETERS FROM 12 TO 30 INCHES ARE APPROPRIATE.

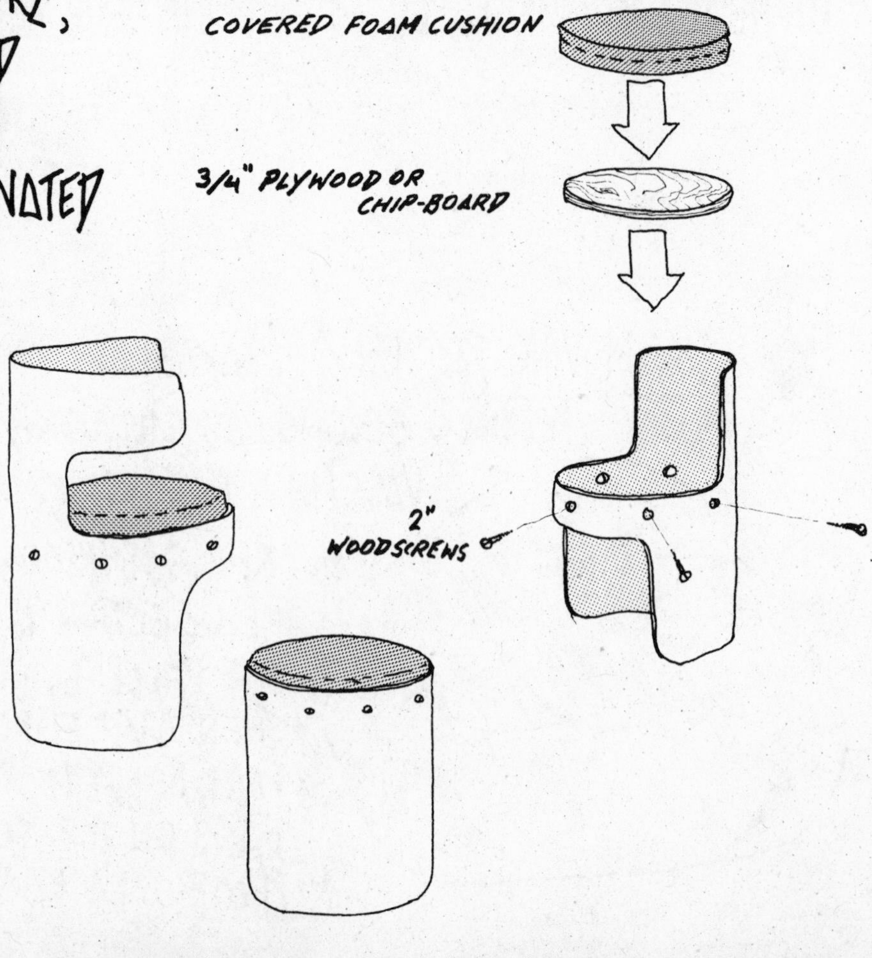

COVERED FOAM CUSHION

3/4" PLYWOOD OR CHIP-BOARD

2" WOODSCREWS

SOME DAY INFLATABLE CHAIRS
THAT WORK, AND ARE
PLEASANT TO SIT ON,
MAY COME INTO
EXISTENCE. AS OF
NOW, THEY ARE
INCONVENIENT, PUT
PEOPLE TOO CLOSE TO
THE FLOOR, SQUEAL LIKE SUCKLING PIGS AT SLAUGHTERING TIME
WHEN RUBBED & HAVE TENDENCIES TO SPRING LEAKS AND
BLOWOUTS. THEY ARE ALSO HOT TO SIT ON FOR ANY LENGTH
OF TIME.

*neoprene-coated nylon.*

BERNARD QUENTIN, DESIGNER.

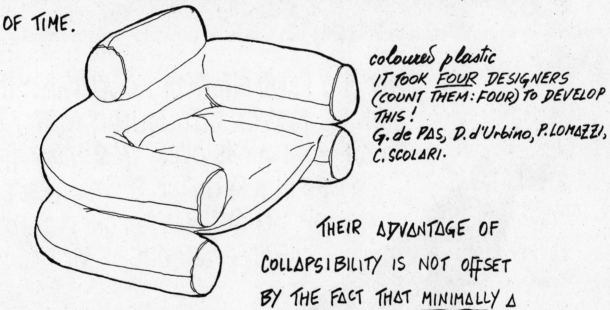

*coloured plastic*
IT TOOK FOUR DESIGNERS
(COUNT THEM: FOUR) TO DEVELOP
THIS!
G. de PAS, D. d'Urbino, P. LOMAZZI,
C. SCOLARI.

THEIR ADVANTAGE OF
COLLAPSIBILITY IS NOT OFFSET
BY THE FACT THAT MINIMALLY A
BICYCLE-PUMP IS NEEDED TO ERECT THEM, A SERVICE STATION
AIR HOSE IS BETTER. THE ONLY THING INFLATABLES SEEM TO
HAVE GOING FOR THEM IS THAT THEY ARE "TRENDY" RIGHT NOW.

*Inflatables*: NONETHELESS THE CONCEPT OF
INFLATABLES IS A GOOD ONE → SOONER OR LATER
A DECENT CHAIR WILL DEVELOP.

THIS IS A RELAXING CHAIR, SO DELICATELY POISED
THAT THE PERSON SITTING IN IT MERELY HAS
TO PUT *HER* ARMS OVER *HER* HEAD [SEE BELOW]
TO BE IN A RELAXING POSITION, FEET UP.
THIS CHAIR WAS DESIGNED BY DOUGLAS
SCHOEFFLER, ONE OF VIC'S STUDENTS

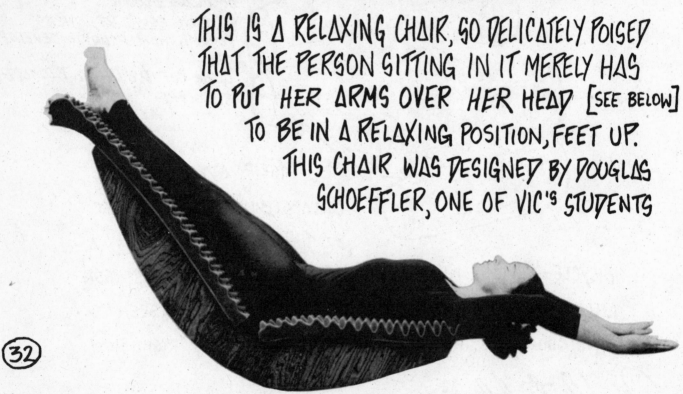

AT THE CALIFORNIA INSTITUTE of THE ARTS. ORIGINALLY DOUGLAS
DESIGNED IT FOR DANCERS & DANCE STUDENTS. BUT OTHERS IN OUR

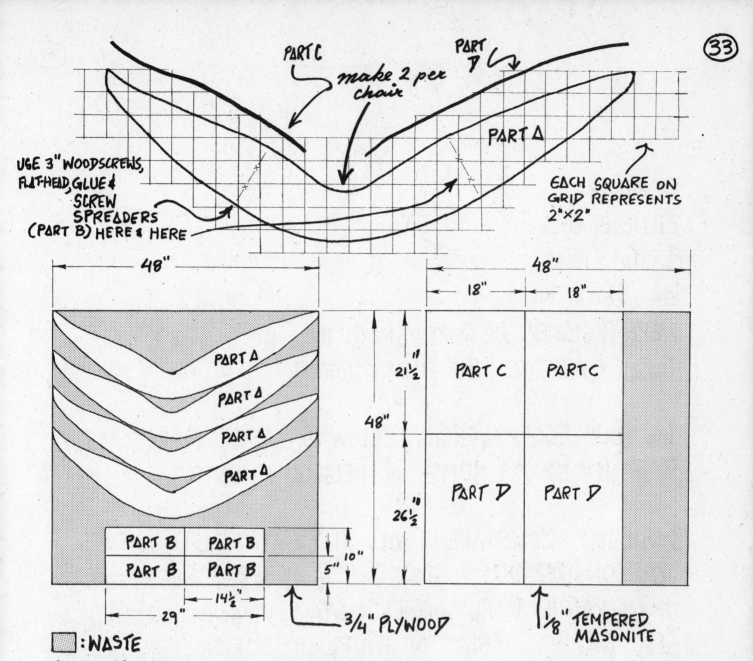

PART C — make 2 per chair

PART D

PART A

USE 3" WOODSCREWS, FLAT-HEAD, GLUE & SCREW SPREADERS (PART B) HERE & HERE

EACH SQUARE ON GRID REPRESENTS 2"×2"

48"

PART A
PART A
PART A
PART A

PART B | PART B
PART B | PART B

29"
14½"
10"
5"

3/4" PLYWOOD

48"

18" | 18"

21½"

PART C | PART C

48"

26½"

PART D | PART D

⅛" TEMPERED MASONITE

▦ : WASTE

SOCIETY NEED TO GET THE EQUIVALENT of 3-4 HOURS of RELAXING TIME IN 1 HOUR: WAITRESSES, NURSES, TEACHERS, ETC.

SO JIM REDESIGNED THE CHAIR AS SHOWN ABOVE. THE TWO PIECES of 48"×48" MATERIALS WILL MAKE TWO CHAIRS IF YOU FOLLOW OUR CUTTING DIAGRAM. FIRST GLUE & SCREW THE TWO SPREADERS [PARTS B] BETWEEN THE TWO OUTSIDE PARTS A. NOW CENTER PARTS C & D OVER STRUCTURE AND, STARTING PART C AT THE TOP & PART D AT THE BOTTOM, GLUE & SCREW TO THE A PARTS OF THE STRUCTURE → USE Nº8 FLAT-HEAD WOODSCREWS, 2" LONG. IF YOU WISH YOU CAN NOW ADD "FINGER-FOAM" PADS [AVAILABLE FROM FOAM MANUFACTURERS].

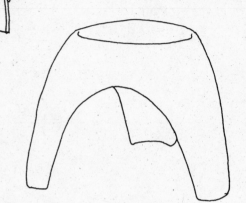

THERE ARE
ZILLIONS OF
PLASTIC STOOLS
THAT STACK. THESE

WERE DESIGNED BY SORI YANAGI IN
JAPAN & ARE AVAILABLE FROM KOTOBUKI.

THE FOUR-LEGGED VERSION BELOW IS MADE f FIBREGLASS,
DESIGNED BY YKI NUMMI of HELSINKI, FINLAND.

BASICALLY STOOLS AREN'T ALL THAT COMFORTABLE. WHEN
YOU CONSIDER THAT A STACK f 4 f EITHER f THESE BEATS
UP & SCRATCHES BADLY WHENEVER STACKED, AND THAT THEY
SELL fo ABOUT $45.- FOR FOUR, WHY BOTHER?

IF YOU FEEL THAT YOU
MUST SIT ON BRIGHTLY
COLOURED, STACKABLE,
PLASTIC UNITS →GO
& BUY PLASTIC BUCKETS
AT YOUR SUPERMARKET,
HARDWARE STORE & CHAIN
DISCOUNT STORE!

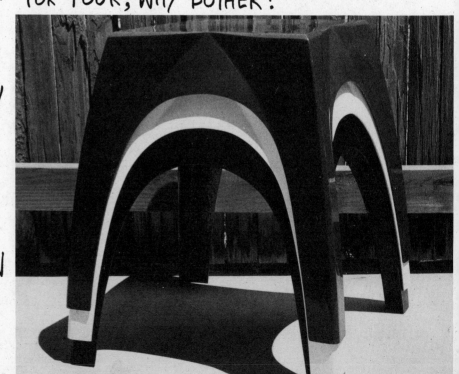

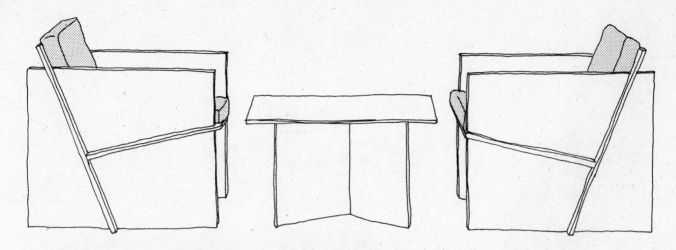

IN 1967 THIS LINE OF FURNITURE, CALLED THE "K-LINE", WAS DESIGNED BY CHRISTOPH IN GERMANY. THE PARTS COME READY~ LAQUERED IN CHARCOAL or WHITE, CUSHIONS ARE AVAILABLE IN MANY COLOUR CHOICES. THEY ARE AVAILABLE FROM ⟶ PAUL KOLD MÖBLER, GL. LAADEGARD, POSTBOX 50, DK-6500, VOJENS, DENMARK.

JIM REDESIGNED THE CHAIR, BELOW:
MAKE IT OF 3/4" PLYWOOD.

Note: NO GLUE, NAILS, SCREWS, or DOWELS ARE NEEDED SINCE THE SLOTS DO ALL THE WORK. COVER THE 2 POLYURETHANE CUSHIONS!

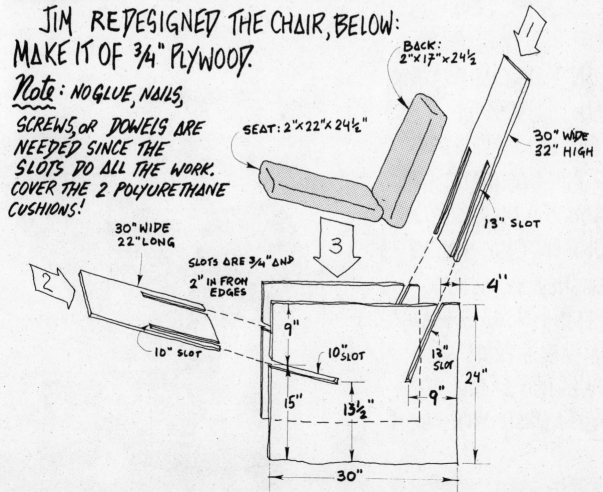

BACK: 2"×17"×24½"

SEAT: 2"×22"×24½"

30" WIDE 32" HIGH

13" SLOT

30" WIDE 22" LONG

SLOTS ARE 3/4" AND 2" IN FROM EDGES

3

2

10" SLOT

9"

10" SLOT

15"

13½"

4"

13" SLOT

24"

9"

30"

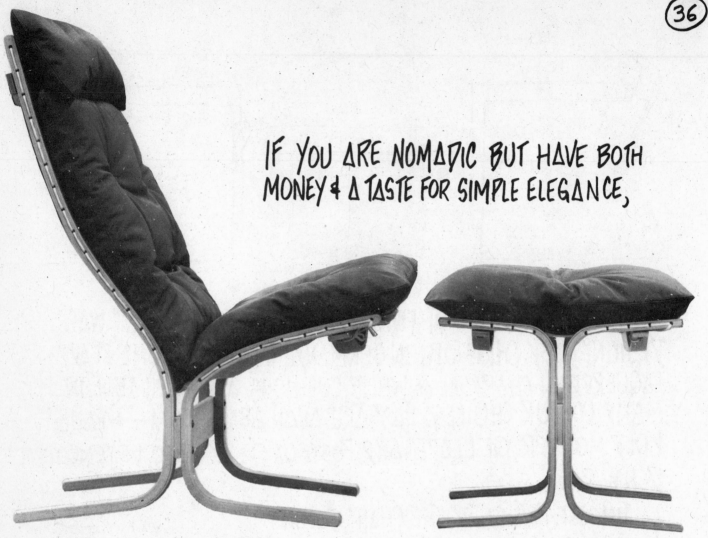

IF YOU ARE NOMADIC BUT HAVE BOTH MONEY & A TASTE FOR SIMPLE ELEGANCE,

THEN THIS CHAIR IS FOR YOU. IT USES THE "FEATHERING" PROPERTY OF THIN, LAMINATED WOOD. AS YOU CAN SEE, IT KNOCKS DOWN FOR EASY MOVING → DESIGNED BY INGMAR RELLING, N.I.L. → AND AVAILABLE FROM: "WESTNOFA" LTD. 6151 ØRSTA, NORWAY. ◄

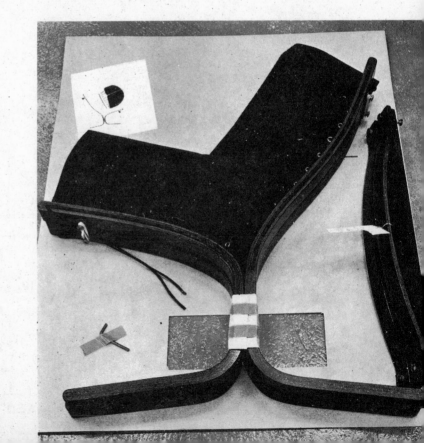

# ADAPTATION BY JIM:

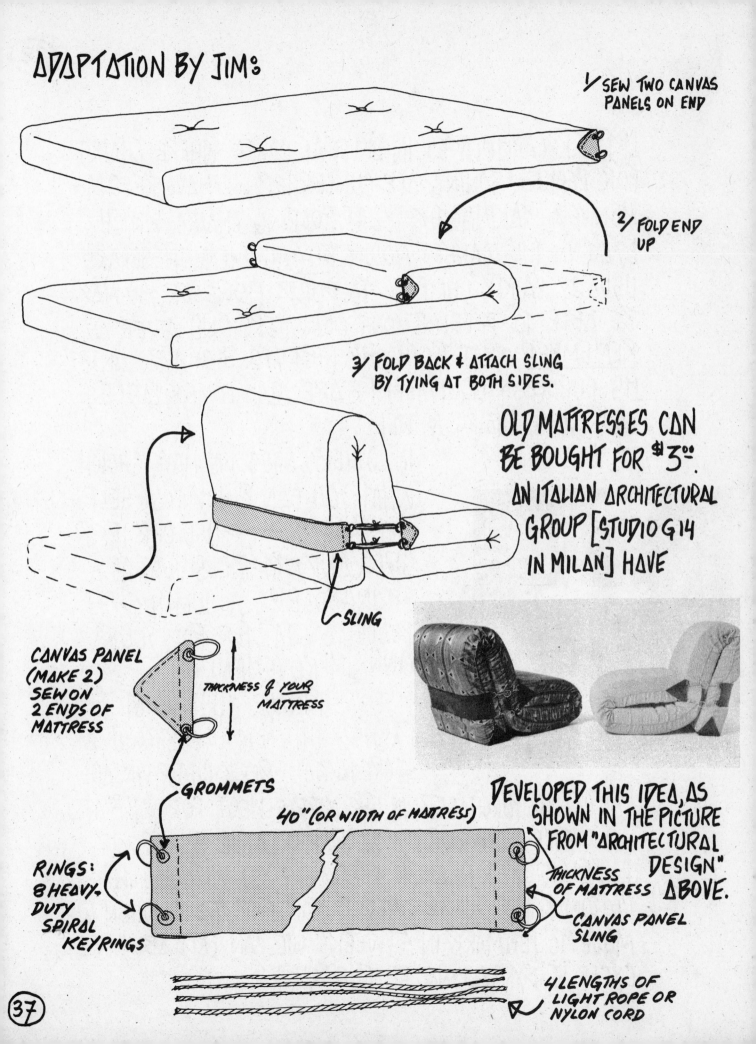

1/ SEW TWO CANVAS PANELS ON END

2/ FOLD END UP

3/ FOLD BACK & ATTACH SLING BY TYING AT BOTH SIDES.

OLD MATTRESSES CAN BE BOUGHT FOR $3⁰⁰. AN ITALIAN ARCHITECTURAL GROUP [STUDIO G14 IN MILAN] HAVE

SLING

CANVAS PANEL (MAKE 2) SEW ON 2 ENDS OF MATTRESS

THICKNESS of YOUR MATTRESS

GROMMETS

40" (OR WIDTH OF MATTRESS)

RINGS: 8 HEAVY-DUTY SPIRAL KEYRINGS

DEVELOPED THIS IDEA, AS SHOWN IN THE PICTURE FROM "ARCHITECTURAL DESIGN" ABOVE.

THICKNESS OF MATTRESS

CANVAS PANEL SLING

4 LENGTHS OF LIGHT ROPE OR NYLON CORD

37

LET'S RECAPITULATE: IN SEVERAL CASES WHERE CHAIRS
FOR DESKS or DINING ARE CONCERNED, WE HAVE RECOM~
MENDED TAKING THE BEST FOLDING CHAIRS WHICH
EXIST IN THE MARKET NOW & <u>BUYING</u> THEM. THESE ARE
USUALLY FAIRLY COMPLEX TO BUILD; HOWEVER, YOU MAY
BE ABLE TO DEVELOP YOUR OWN VERSIONS AFTER ALL.
<u>REMEMBER</u> THAT BOTH THE DIRECTORS CHAIR AND
ITS EUROPEAN EQUIVALENTS ARE ALSO COMFORTABLE
LOUNGING CHAIRS AS WELL.

IN OTHER CASES WE HAVE SHOWN
WHAT YOU CAN BUILD YOURSELF.
HERE AGAIN ——→ USE OUR IDEAS,
SIZES, AND MATERIALS JUST AS A
SPRINGBOARD: A JUMPING-OFF
PLACE, A STARTER FOR YOUR
OWN IMPROVEMENTS.

FINALLY: USE WHAT
EXISTS! THIS PICTURE SHOWS A
SECRETARIAL DESK CHAIR, VINTAGE
1907, AND PURCHASED IN THE MIDDLE~WEST FOR $1⁰⁰ AT
AN OFFICE BANKRUPTCY SALE. HARLANNE PAINTED IT
IN BRIGHT RED ENAMEL & RECOVERED IT WITH A marimekko
COTTON PRINT. WE'VE USED IT FOR FIVE YEARS, WHEN WE
MOVE TO DENMARK IN 5 WEEKS, WE CAN PROBABLY RE~
CYCLE IT BY SELLING IT FOR $2⁰⁰!

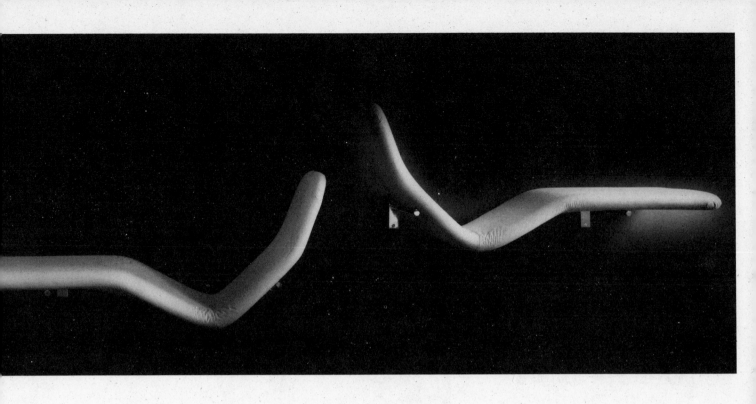

AND FINALLY A REALLY FAR-OUT CONCEPT
IN SEATING: EXPERIMENTAL WALL~SUPPORTED LOUNGE CHAIRS. THESE
WERE DESIGNED SEVERAL YEARS AGO BY OUR FRIEND ANTTI
NURMESNIEMI, A LEADING INDUSTRIAL DESIGNER IN HELSINKI.
THEY ARE INCLUDED HERE FOR SEVERAL FRANKLY SPECULATIVE
REASONS: PROVIDED THE WALLS & WALL~ANCHORS ARE STRONG
ENOUGH ~ COULD THE CHAIRS' POSITIONS BE VARIED?
COULD THIS JUST BE USED AS A WALL-STORAGE METHOD
[SIMILAR TO THE SHAKERS, WHO HUNG THEIR CHAIRS ON THE
WALLS WHEN NOT USED]? HOW WOULD A MODIFICATION
OF DOUGLAS SCHOEFFLER'S LOUNGING CHAIR [PAGE 33] WORK
IN THIS SET~UP?

THE SPECULATIVE QUESTIONS ARE ENDLESS:
HOW ELSE COULD ONE SIT ON A WALL? CAN SEATS HANG FROM
STANDING BOOKCASES & STORAGE SYSTEMS? OR IS THE
NOMADIC IDEAL TO HAVE 2 FOAM PADS IN ONE'S HIP~POCKETS &
SIT ANYWHERE → YOUR SLACKS AS AN EASY~CHAIR?

(39)

## Simplest Support:

PROBABLY THE SIMPLEST
SUPPORT STRUCTURE
THAT CAN BE BUILT
OUT of CORRUGATED
CARDBOARD, THAT IS
ALSO SELF~FASTENING
[NO GLUE or FASTENERS
or TAPE] IS THIS.→
WHEN MOVING IT
FOLDS ABSOLUTELY
FLAT. IT WILL SUPPORT

UP TO 400 POUNDS. YOU CAN CHANGE THE HEIGHT & WIDTH
DIMENSIONS AND USE IT TO SUPPORT BEDS, TABLES, DESKS,
CHAIRS, STOOLS, ETC.→ SEE ALSO PAGE 49.

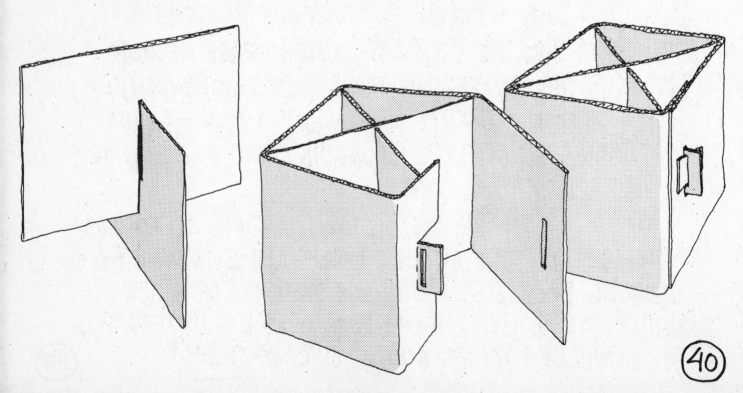

# EATING + WORKING:

EATING IN BED CAN BE FUN. AND WORK of COURSE IS CARRIED OUT UNDER ALL KINDS of CONDITIONS, AND IN MANY ODD PLACES.

BUT FOR THE PURPOSES OF THIS SECTION, WE ARE TALKING ABOUT EATING AT TABLES. THE KIND OF WORK~SURFACES THAT WE ARE CONCERNED WITH ARE DESK TOPS, WORKBENCHES AND THE KIND of DRAWING SURFACES THAT A DESIGNER, ARTIST or DRAUGHTS-MAN WOULD NEED. THESE LATTER, THE DRAWING TABLES, ARE SOMETIMES AT DESK~HEIGHT, SOMETIMES AT THE CORRECT HEIGHT FOR TALLER STOOLS. STILL OTHER PEOPLE [VIC & JIM FOR INSTANCE] PREFER TO STAND WHILE DRAUGHTING.

MOST BOOKS THAT DEAL WITH HUMAN MEASUREMENTS ADVOCATE "STANDARD DINING TABLE HEIGHT" of 30" or SOMETIMES, 29½". IN FACT, MOST STORE~BOUGHT TABLES ARE THAT TALL. WE ADVOCATE THAT TABLES OUGHT TO BE DRASTICALLY LOWER, ANYWHERE BETWEEN 27½" TO 28¾". IN ONE SPECIAL CASE, WE

HAVE EVEN MADE A CASE FOR A DINING TABLE THAT IS ONLY 23½ INCHES TALL.

WORKING WITH DIFFERENT TYPES OF DRAWING TABLES, WE HAVE BOTH FOUND THAT THE ANGLE ADJUST~ MENT FOR THE TABLE SURFACE IS USED VERY LITTLE. MOST PEOPLE WILL FIND AN ANGLE THAT SEEMS COMFORTABLE TO THEM, AND THEN LEAVE IT LIKE THAT "FOREVER". YOU CAN EXPERIMENT WITH VARYING ANGLES [BY PROPPING UP THE FAR SIDE OF A PLYWOOD BOARD WITH SOME BOOKS], AND THEN KNOW WHAT YOUR PERSONAL PREFERENCE IS. THEN CHANGE OUR DESIGN SUGGESTIONS TO YOUR "IDEAL" ANGLE.

SOMEONE ONCE DEFINED A TABLE AS "AN EXTENSION OF THE FLOOR". WE FEEL CERTAIN THAT IF YOU THINK OF EATING & WORKING TABLES IN THAT LIGHT, YOU CAN MAKE YOUR OWN VARIATIONS ON THE IDEAS WE HAVE DEVELOPED HERE.

AGAIN: WHAT WE HAVE SELECTED IN THIS CHAPTER REPRESENTS A GOOD CROSS~SECTION OF THOSE THINGS YOU CAN EASILY BUILD OR BUY, THINGS THAT MAKE SENSE IN TERMS OF A NOMADIC LIFE~STYLE. BY NO MEANS HAVE WE SUCCEEDED IN LISTING EVERYTHING.

MATERIALS, SUPPLIES, TOOLS & SKILLS WILL BE AS DIFFERENT AS YOUR NEEDS.

THAT'S WHERE YOU COME IN!

# Drop-Down Table:

WHEN SPACE IS AT A PREMIUM THIS TABLE [OR DESK] MAKES SENSE. WHEN NOT IN USE, BOTH THE TABLE SURFACE & THE LEG FOLD FLAT BACK INTO THE WALL-FRAME.

PHOTO~ MURAL OR PAINTING

54"

32"

23½"

12"

THE FRAME IS MADE FROM 2"×4" LUMBER, (YOU'LL NEED ONE 6 FOOT AND TWO 8 FOOT LENGTHS), MITRE~CUT TO FIT AROUND THE 32"×54" TABLE TOP. BOLT FRAME TO WALL BEFORE ATTACHING TABLE TOP.

THIS TABLE LEG IS 27" TALL AND SET IN 12½" FROM THE FRONT EDGE. IT IS CENTERED AND ATTACHED WITH 2 MEDIUM-SIZED HINGES

WHEN VIC BUILT A TABLE LIKE THIS IN A ONE-ROOM OFFICE IN CANADA, HE ALSO CUT A PIECE OF FOAM~CORE BOARD JUST A MILLIMETER LARGER THAN 32"×54". HE COULD THEN PLACE THIS WHITE FOAM~CORE SHEET IN FRONT OF THE FOLDED~UP TABLE WITHIN THE WALL FRAME, AND USE ONE SIDE AS A PIN-BOARD, THE OTHER AS A PROJECTION SCREEN FOR SLIDES.

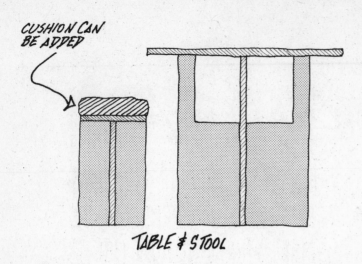

CUSHION CAN BE ADDED

TABLE & STOOL

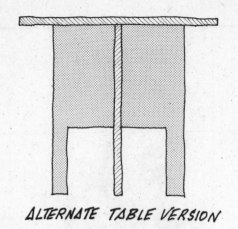

ALTERNATE TABLE VERSION

JIM USES THIS TABLE AND FOUR STOOLS IN HIS HOME. AS YOU CAN SEE, IT IS REALLY THE MOST MINIMAL METHOD OF SOLVING THE PROBLEM.

NO GLUE, NAILS, SCREWS OR FASTENERS ARE NEEDED FOR THE BASIC "X"-SHAPED UNDERSTRUCTURE. WE RECOMMEND THAT YOU USE SMALL ANGLE-BRACKETS & FLAT-HEAD WOODSCREWS TO ATTACH THE TABLE TOPS AND THE SEATS OF THE STOOLS TO THE BOTTOM "X". WHEN MOVING, YOU CAN JUST UNSCREW THEM AND THEN SLIDE THE WOODEN PIECES APART.

→ INSTEAD OF PLYWOOD, YOU CAN USE CHIP-BOARD, FINISH THE EDGES WITH TAPE AND PAINT THE UNITS. YOU MIGHT NAIL FURNITURE GLIDES INTO ALL BOTTOM EDGES.

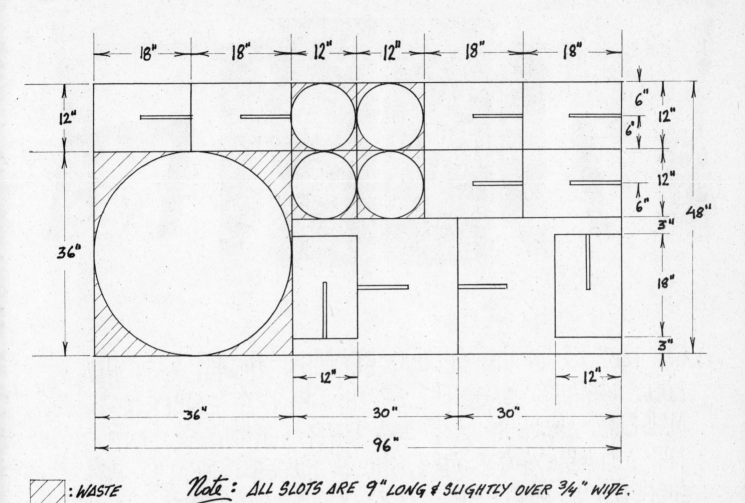

☐ : WASTE    *Note* : ALL SLOTS ARE 9" LONG & SLIGHTLY OVER ¾" WIDE.

➤ BY FOLLOWING OUR CUTTING DIAGRAM [ABOVE] YOU CAN GET EITHER OF THE TWO TABLE VERSIONS, AS WELL AS FOUR STOOLS, OUT OF A STANDARD 4×8-FOOT SHEET OF PLYWOOD. USE ¾" OR ¹⁵⁄₁₆" PLYWOOD. IF YOU WANT TO ADD CUSHIONS, YOU CAN GET POLYURETHANE FOAM, PRE~CUT AS "BAR STOOL TOPS" & COVER THEM IN WHATEVER FABRIC PLEASES YOU. THE TABLE & STOOLS KNOCK DOWN INTO A NEAT, FLAT PACKAGE & ARE EASY TO TRANS~ PORT. ➤ IF YOU WISH, YOU NEED NOT REMOVE THE FOUR WASTE AREAS AROUND THE TABLE [CROSS-HATCHED IN THE ABOVE DIAGRAM], AND YOU'LL HAVE A SQUARE TABLE. YOU COULD ALSO HAVE SQUARE STOOLS BY THE SAME METHOD.

ON PAGE 23 IN THE "SEATING" SECTION OF THIS BOOK, WE HAVE
FULLY DESCRIBED ARCHITECT FRANK GEHRY'S "EASY EDGES"
MATERIAL. ABOVE IS A DINING TABLE SEATING SIX AND
ITS ACCOMPANYING CHAIRS. THESE PIECES ARE ALSO DE~
SIGNED AND MARKETED BY GEHRY'S FIRM IN SANTA MONICA.
THE TABLE SELLS FOR ABOUT $100.— [IT IS SO WELL
STRUCTURED THAT IT CAN SUPPORT ABOUT 1000 POUNDS], THE
CHAIRS ARE LESS THAN $30.— EACH.

THIS IS A CASE WHERE THE UNUSUAL SOUND~
ABSORBING PROPERTIES, AT THE SOURCE, OF THIS MATERIAL
COME TO BE VERY HANDY IN REDUCING THE CLATTER OF
DISHES.

WE SHOW IT HERE BOTH AS AN EXCELLENT EXAMPLE
OF DESIGN MADE FROM "WASTE", WHICH YOU MIGHT BUY, AS
WELL AS A CONCEPT OF LAMINATION FROM WHICH YOU
MIGHT DEVELOP YOUR OWN DESIGN IDEAS.

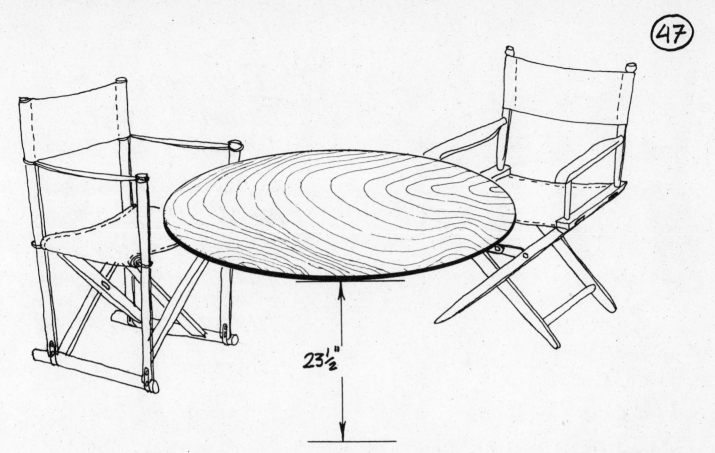

23½"

WHILE WE ARE NOT TRYING TO LOWER TABLE HEIGHTS TOO
DRASTICALLY, THERE ARE SPECIAL CASES WHEN AN UNUSUALLY
LOW TABLE MAKES SENSE. INGELISE BRATVOLD & GEORG JEDDE,
WHO PUBLISH "MOBILIA" MAGAZINE IN DENMARK, HAVE
A VERY INFORMAL LOW TABLE, SURROUNDED BY FOLDING
SWEDISH DIRECTORS CHAIRS. THIS TABLE IS ONLY 23½"
TALL, AND SERVES EXCELLENTLY FOR BREAKFASTS, BRUNCHES
OR RELAXED SUPPERS WITH FRIENDS.

THE TABLE IS ROUND AND HAS A DIAMETER OF 51½
INCHES AND THUS ACCOMMODATES FOUR PEOPLE SO EASILY
THAT SIX AND, IN A PINCH, EVEN EIGHT PEOPLE CAN SIT
AROUND IT.

→ AS 51½" IS WIDER THAN THE 48" STOCK PLYWOOD
WIDTH, WE SUGGEST THAT IT CAN BE CUT OF 2 SEMI-CIRCLES.
AS TO HOW TO SUPPORT A TABLE-TOP [AT ANY HEIGHT]:

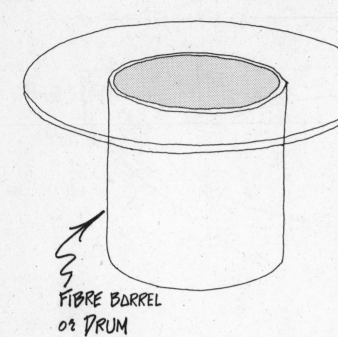

FIBRE BARREL
OR DRUM

NOTE: ON THIS & THE
FOLLOWING PAGE, ALL
TABLE~TOPS ARE SHOWN
AS TRANSPARENT, SO THAT
YOU CAN SEE THE SUPPORT
STRUCTURES CLEARLY. FOR
THESE EXAMPLES WE HAVE
ASSUMED ROUND TOPS, 36" IN
DIAMETER & HEIGHTS OF $27\frac{1}{2}$"

FIVE FIBRE TUBES,
CARDBOARD MAILING
TUBES, ETC. YOU CAN
EPOXY THEM TOGETHER
OR USE TAPE, THEN
PAINT.

YOU CAN, OF COURSE,
SUBSTITUTE SQUARE OR
HEXAGONAL TOPS.

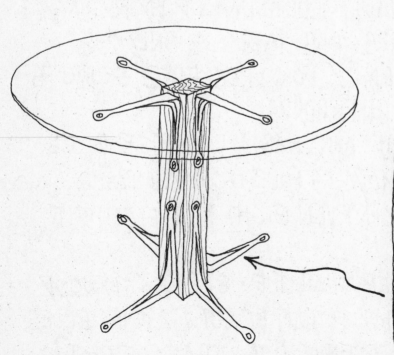

USE EIGHT LARGE-SIZE
ANGLE BRACKETS, SCREW
INTO $3\frac{5}{8}$" × $3\frac{5}{8}$" WOOD.
PAINT.

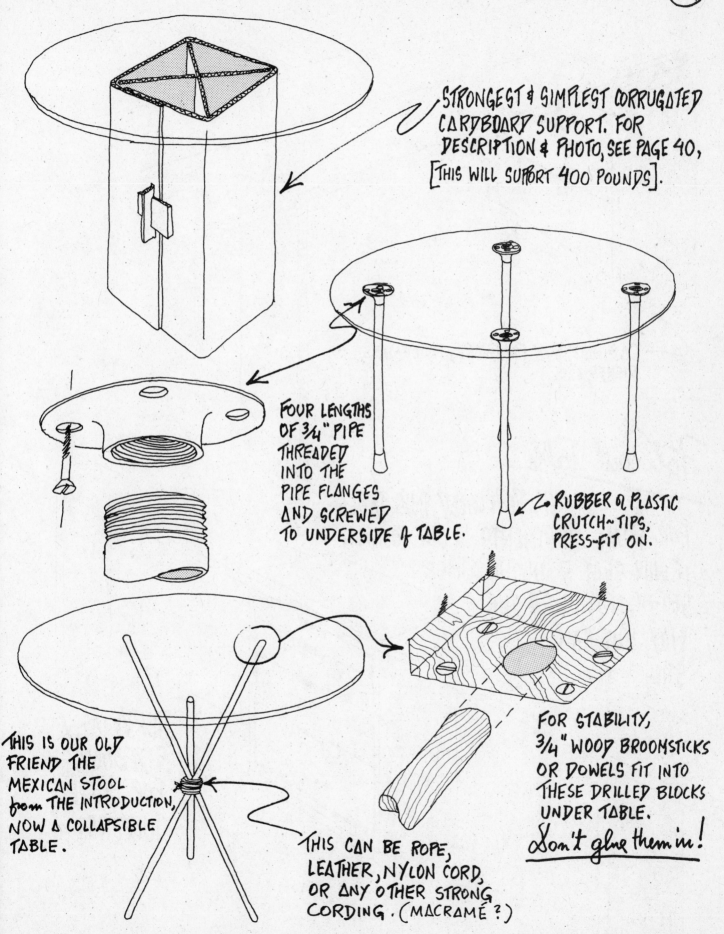

STRONGEST & SIMPLEST CORRUGATED CARDBOARD SUPPORT. FOR DESCRIPTION & PHOTO, SEE PAGE 40, [THIS WILL SUPPORT 400 POUNDS].

FOUR LENGTHS OF 3/4" PIPE THREADED INTO THE PIPE FLANGES AND SCREWED TO UNDERSIDE OF TABLE.

RUBBER or PLASTIC CRUTCH~TIPS, PRESS-FIT ON.

FOR STABILITY, 3/4" WOOD BROOMSTICKS OR DOWELS FIT INTO THESE DRILLED BLOCKS UNDER TABLE. Don't glue them in!

THIS IS OUR OLD FRIEND THE MEXICAN STOOL from THE INTRODUCTION, NOW A COLLAPSIBLE TABLE.

THIS CAN BE ROPE, LEATHER, NYLON CORD, OR ANY OTHER STRONG CORDING. (MACRAMÉ?)

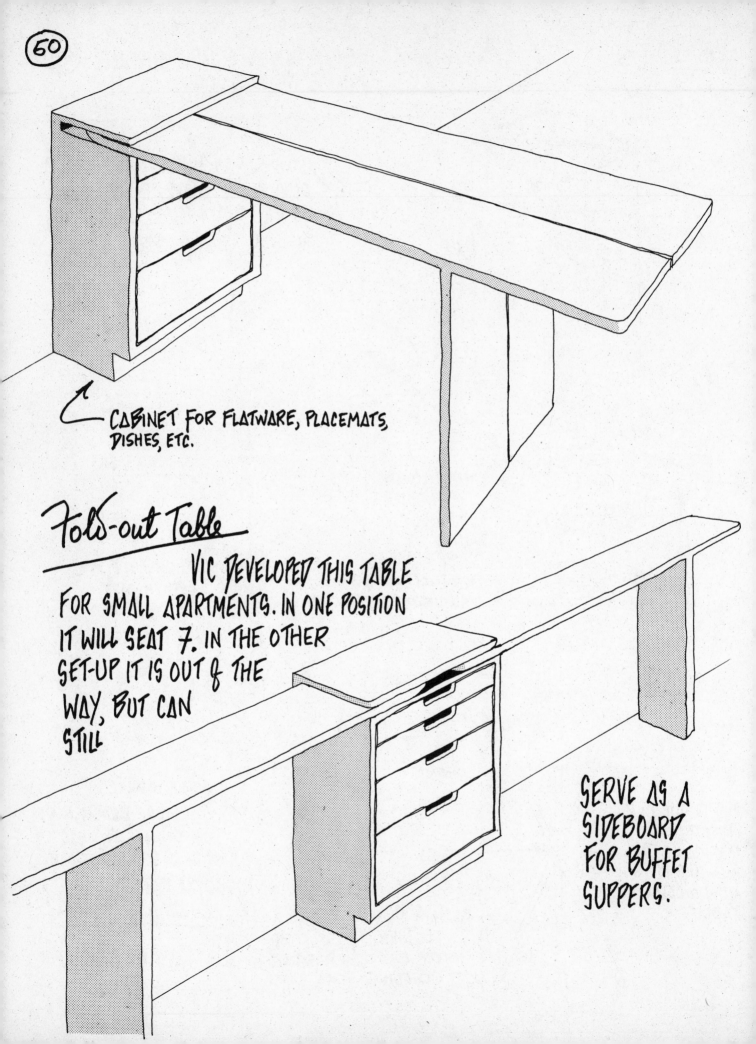

↰ CABINET FOR FLATWARE, PLACEMATS, DISHES, ETC.

## Fold-out Table

VIC DEVELOPED THIS TABLE FOR SMALL APARTMENTS. IN ONE POSITION IT WILL SEAT 7. IN THE OTHER SET-UP IT IS OUT OF THE WAY, BUT CAN STILL

SERVE AS A SIDEBOARD FOR BUFFET SUPPERS.

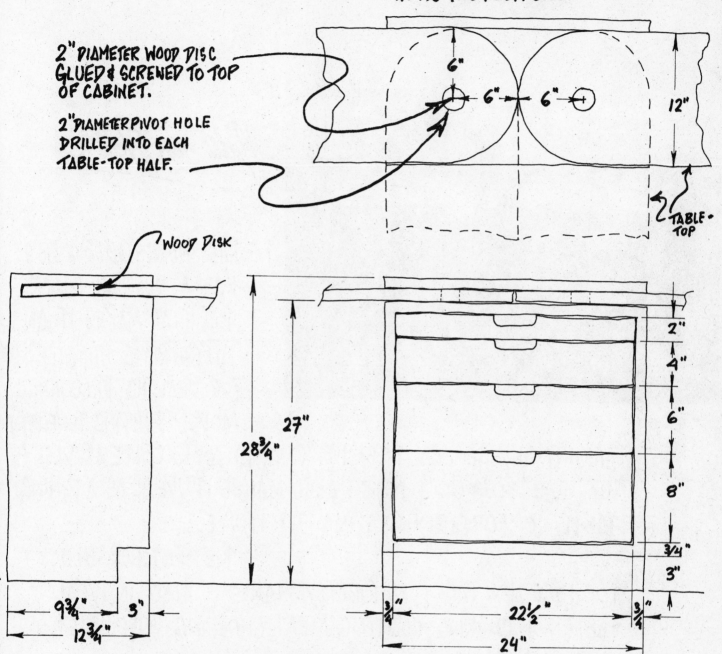

2" DIAMETER WOOD DISC
GLUED & SCREWED TO TOP
OF CABINET.

2" DIAMETER PIVOT HOLE
DRILLED INTO EACH
TABLE-TOP HALF.

WOOD DISK

TABLE-TOP

WE SUGGEST 4 DRAWERS, AS SHOWN. BUT YOU MAY
PREFER OPEN SHELVING, OR CABINET DOORS, WHAT~
EVER.

ASSUMED MATERIAL IS ¾" PLYWOOD, PAINTED.

YOU CAN BUY ALUMINUM "L" EXTRUSIONS AT THE HARDWARE
STORE & MOUNT THEM HORIZONTALLY IN THE CABINET AS
DRAWER GLIDES.

## Multi~use Table:

THIS WORK~TABLE of VIC'S HAS A BUTCHER~BLOCK TOP. THAT MAKES IT AN APPROPRIATE SURFACE FOR DRAWING, DRAUGHTING, MODEL~BUILDING, JEWELLERY MAKING AND GENERAL DESK WORK. IT IS AN EXCELLENT DESK~TOP SIZE [30" × 60"], WHICH ALSO MAKES IT IDEAL AS A DINING TABLE, COMFORTABLY SEATING SIX PEOPLE.

THE BUTCHER~BLOCK TOP [SEE NEXT PAGE], NATURALLY MAKES IT ALSO AN IDEAL TABLE FOR COOKING, CUTTING MEAT, CHOPPING VEGETABLES or ROLLING OUT DOUGH.

SINCE THE TOP IS SECURED TO THE TWO CHROMED SAWHORSES WITH ONLY FOUR 2½" WOODSCREWS, THE WHOLE THING COMES APART FOR EASY MOVING ~ [CAUTION → THE SAME WEIGHT THAT KEEPS THE TOP FROM MOVING, ALSO MAKES IT VERY HEAVY. THAT'S A CHARACTERISTIC of WOOD LAMINATES].

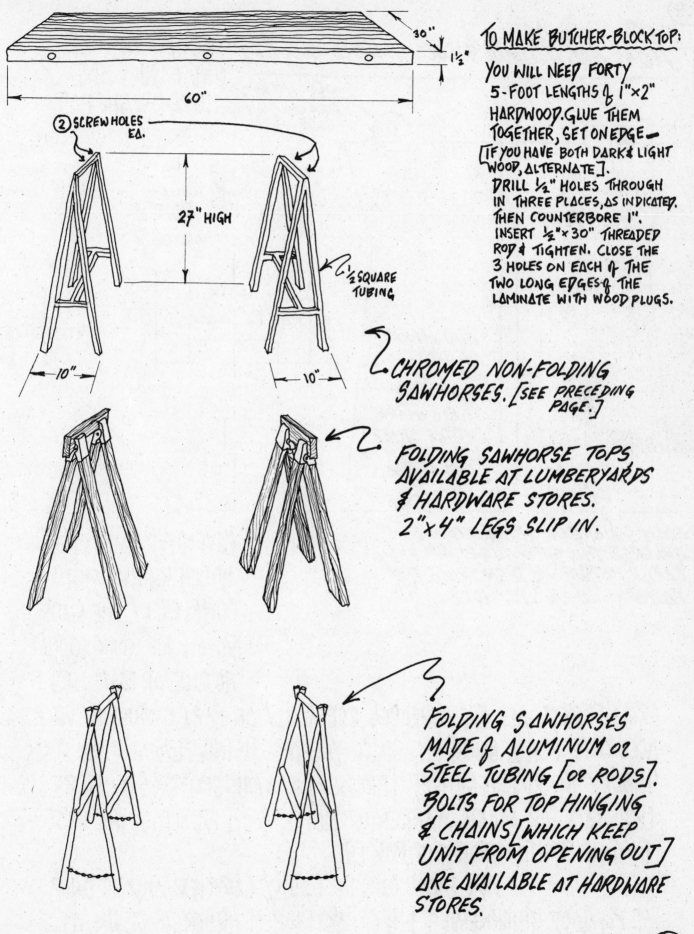

60"

30"

1½"

② SCREW HOLES
EA.

27" HIGH

½" SQUARE
TUBING

10"    10"

TO MAKE BUTCHER-BLOCK TOP:

YOU WILL NEED FORTY
5-FOOT LENGTHS of 1"×2"
HARDWOOD. GLUE THEM
TOGETHER, SET ON EDGE.
[IF YOU HAVE BOTH DARK & LIGHT
WOOD, ALTERNATE].
DRILL ½" HOLES THROUGH
IN THREE PLACES, AS INDICATED.
THEN COUNTERBORE 1".
INSERT ½"× 30" THREADED
ROD & TIGHTEN. CLOSE THE
3 HOLES ON EACH of THE
TWO LONG EDGES of THE
LAMINATE WITH WOOD PLUGS.

CHROMED NON-FOLDING
SAWHORSES. [SEE PRECEDING
PAGE.]

FOLDING SAWHORSE TOPS,
AVAILABLE AT LUMBERYARDS
& HARDWARE STORES.
2"×4" LEGS SLIP IN.

FOLDING SAWHORSES
MADE of ALUMINUM or
STEEL TUBING [or RODS].
BOLTS FOR TOP HINGING
& CHAINS [WHICH KEEP
UNIT FROM OPENING OUT]
ARE AVAILABLE AT HARDWARE
STORES.

53

# *Nan del Monte's collapsible stool:*

NAN DEL MONTE IS ONE of JIM & VIC'S STUDENTS. SHE HAS

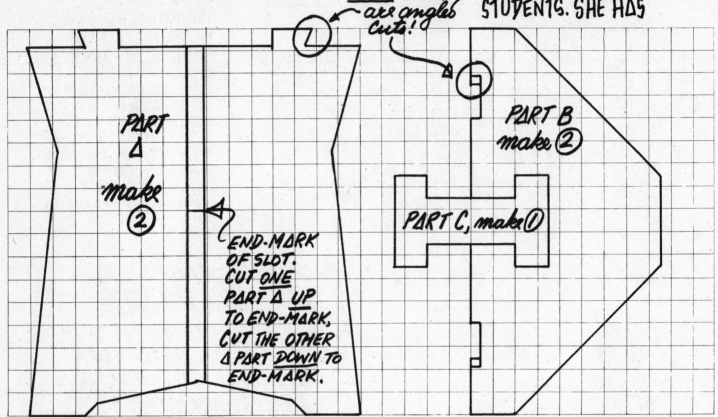

note: these are angled cuts!

PART A make (2)

END-MARK OF SLOT. CUT ONE PART A UP TO END-MARK, CUT THE OTHER A PART DOWN TO END-MARK.

PART B make (2)

PART C, make (1)

EACH SQUARE ON GRID EQUALS 1"x1" ENLARGE THIS GRID TO GET A FULL-SIZE PAPER PATTERN & THEN TRACE THE PATTERNS ON 3/4" PLYWOOD.

DEVELOPED THIS STOOL WHICH KNOCKS DOWN COMPLETELY. THE SLOTS DO ALL THE WORK, SO THAT NO GLUE OR FASTENERS ARE NEEDED. ALL THE SURFACES, ESPECIALLY ON PART C, MUST BE VERY ACCURATE FOR A SNUG FIT. SINCE YOU ARE USING PLYWOOD ALL EDGES SHOULD BE FINISH~SANDED [DRESSED] TO AVOID SPLITS & SPLINTERS. USE TAPE OR MAGIC MARKER OR NOTCHES TO IDENTIFY THE BEST FITTING POSITION FOR THE PARTS.

HER STOOL CAN BE EASILY CARRIED AND IS ONLY 4 PLYWOOD THICKNESSES WIDE [2½"] WHEN KNOCKED DOWN, AT MOST.

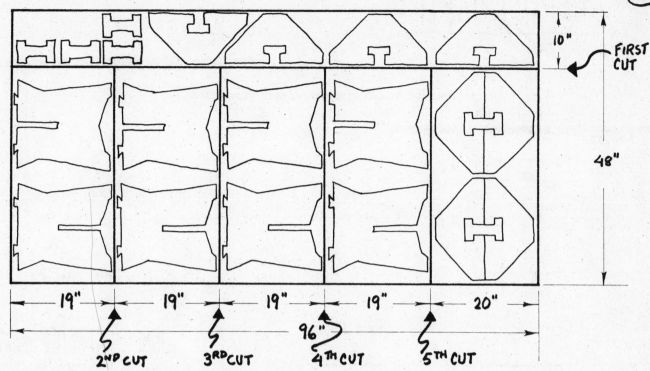

10"

FIRST CUT

48"

19"    19"    19"    19"    20"

96"

2ND CUT    3RD CUT    4TH CUT    5TH CUT

YOU CAN MAKE FOUR OF THESE STOOLS OUT OF A STANDARD SHEET OF PLYWOOD [4×8 FEET], BY FOLLOWING OUR CUTTING DIAGRAM ABOVE. FIRST RIP-CUT THE 10" STRIP OFF, THEN MAKE THE OTHER FOUR CUTS. THIS WILL LEAVE YOU WITH PIECES THAT ARE MORE MANAGEABLE IN SIZE FOR THE MORE PRECISE CUTTING. YOU MUST BE PRECISE TO HAVE THIS STOOL WORK.

# 3~HEIGHT TABLE:

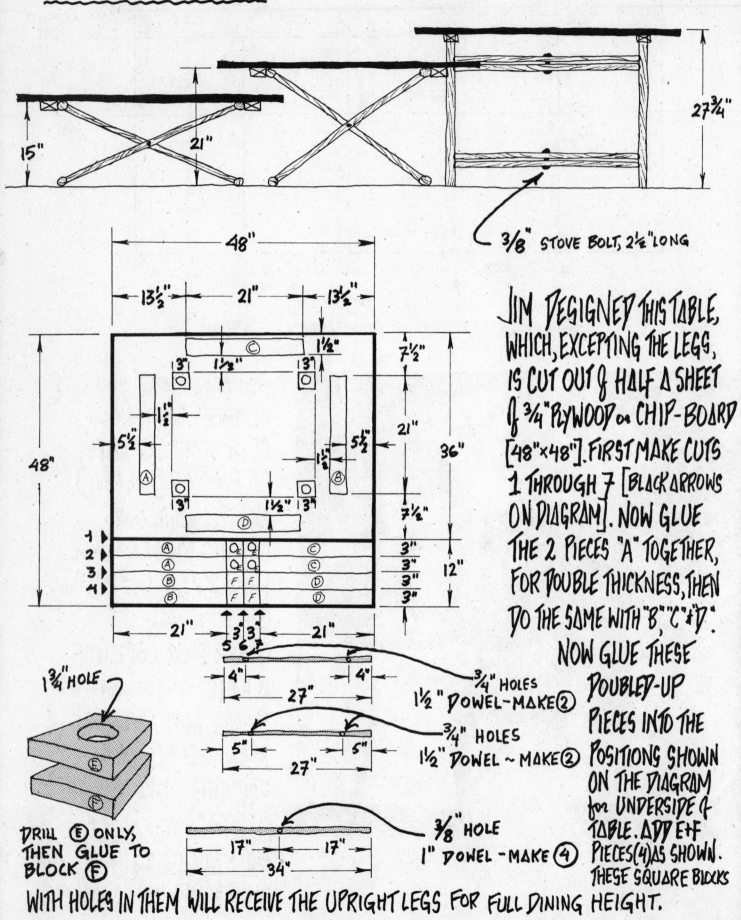

27¾"

15"  21"

3/8" STOVE BOLT, 2½" LONG

48"

13½"  21"  13½"

1½"
3"  1½"  3"
1½"
C
5½"  1½"  5½"
A  B
3"  1½"  3"
D

7½"
21"  36"
7½"
12"

1  ▸
2  ▸  A  O E  O E  C  3"
3  ▸  A  O E  O E  C  3"
4  ▸  B  F  F  D  3"
     B  F  F  D  3"

48"

21"  3"3"  21"
5 6 7

¾" HOLES
4"  4"  1½" DOWEL—MAKE ②
27"

¾" HOLES
5"  5"  1½" DOWEL ~ MAKE ②
27"

1¾" HOLE

E
F

DRILL E ONLY,
THEN GLUE TO
BLOCK F

17"  17"  ⅜" HOLE
34"  1" DOWEL –MAKE ④

JIM DESIGNED THIS TABLE, WHICH, EXCEPTING THE LEGS, IS CUT OUT OF HALF A SHEET OF ¾" PLYWOOD OR CHIP-BOARD [48"×48"]. FIRST MAKE CUTS 1 THROUGH 7 [BLACK ARROWS ON DIAGRAM]. NOW GLUE THE 2 PIECES "A" TOGETHER, FOR DOUBLE THICKNESS, THEN DO THE SAME WITH "B" "C" & "D".

NOW GLUE THESE DOUBLED-UP PIECES INTO THE POSITIONS SHOWN ON THE DIAGRAM for UNDERSIDE of TABLE. ADD E&F PIECES(4)AS SHOWN. THESE SQUARE BLOCKS

WITH HOLES IN THEM WILL RECEIVE THE UPRIGHT LEGS FOR FULL DINING HEIGHT.

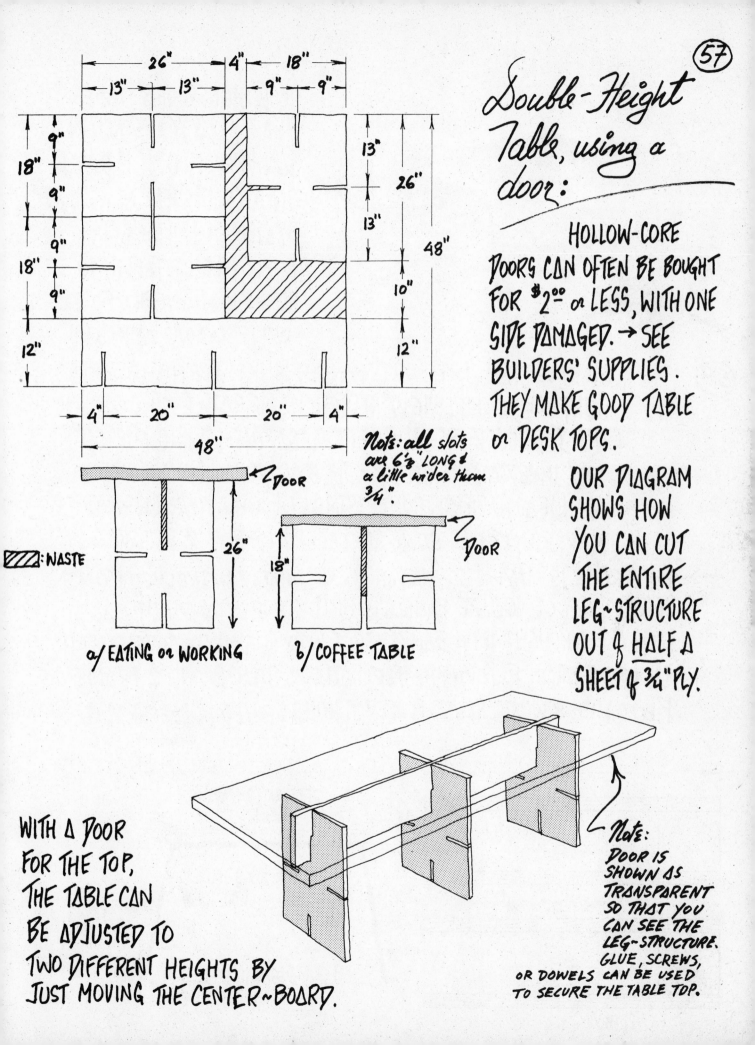

# Double-Height Table, using a door:

HOLLOW-CORE DOORS CAN OFTEN BE BOUGHT FOR $2.00 or LESS, WITH ONE SIDE DAMAGED. → SEE BUILDERS' SUPPLIES. THEY MAKE GOOD TABLE or DESK TOPS.

OUR DIAGRAM SHOWS HOW YOU CAN CUT THE ENTIRE LEG~STRUCTURE OUT of HALF A SHEET of 3/4" PLY.

26"  13"  13"  4"  18"  9"  9"

18"  9"  9"

13"  26"  13"  48"

18"  9"  9"

10"

12"  12"

4"  20"  20"  4"

48"

Note: all slots are 6½" LONG & a little wider than 3/4".

DOOR

26"

a/ EATING or WORKING

DOOR

18"

b/ COFFEE TABLE

⊟ : WASTE

WITH A DOOR FOR THE TOP, THE TABLE CAN BE ADJUSTED TO TWO DIFFERENT HEIGHTS BY JUST MOVING THE CENTER~BOARD.

Note: DOOR IS SHOWN AS TRANSPARENT SO THAT YOU CAN SEE THE LEG~STRUCTURE. GLUE, SCREWS, OR DOWELS CAN BE USED TO SECURE THE TABLE TOP.

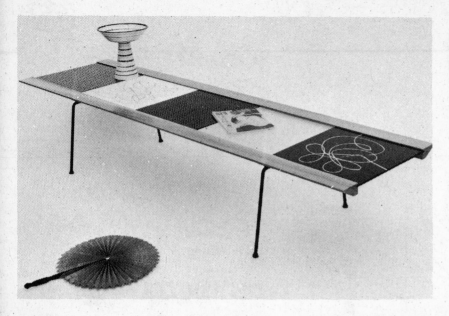

VIC DESIGNED THIS TABLE NEARLY 20 YEARS AGO IN SAN FRANCISCO. IT IS BASED ON A COMPLETELY NEW SYSTEM OF HOLDING THE 5-FOOT-LONG TABLE TOGETHER WITH ONLY 8 WOODSCREWS, AND STILL

(58) MAKING THE 1×1-FOOT PANELS, WHICH FORM THE TABLE SURFACE, COMPLETELY INTERCHANGEABLE. THE DESIGN WAS PUBLISHED BY "SUNSET" MAGAZINE DURING THE 50$, AND IMMEDIATELY RIPPED-OFF BY SEVERAL FURNITURE MANUFACTURERS. SURPRISINGLY FOR FAST-CHANGING MARKETS, IT HAS SOLD SUCCESSFULLY FOR 2 DECADES.

→ THE FRAME IS MADE of 2 WOODEN 2"×3"s, SHAPED & GROOVED TO RECEIVE THE FOOT-SQUARE PANELS, WHICH SLIDE IN AND OUT EASILY. LEGS ARE WROUGHT IRON BANDS, BENT INTO SLIGHTLY OUTWARD SLOPED U's & BENT AGAIN TO FORM THE FEET. ATTACH THEM TO THE 2 FRAME PIECES WITH 8 WOODSCREWS, PLACED IN HOLES DRILLED IN CORNERS of U.

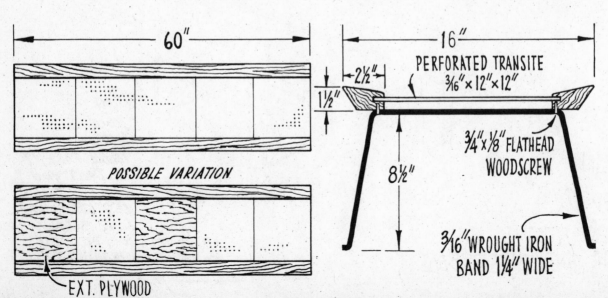

60"

POSSIBLE VARIATION

EXT. PLYWOOD

16"

PERFORATED TRANSITE
3/16"×12"×12"

2½"

1½"

8½"

3/4"×1/8" FLATHEAD WOODSCREW

3/16" WROUGHT IRON BAND 1/4" WIDE

AS YOU CAN SEE, THE 3/16" PANELS, DON'T HAVE TO BE PERFORATED TRANSITE, PAINTED MASONITE, WOOD or GLASS.

YOU CAN MAKE FOAM SEAT~PADS, PLANT~BOXES, RECORDING & HI-FI INSTALLATIONS, OUT~SIZE ASHTRAYS, RIPPLED GLASS PANELS, SHADOW~BOXES THAT ARE GLASS-TOPPED & LIT FROM BELOW TO DISPLAY YOUR COLLECTION of SEASHELLS or WHAT-HAVE-YOU. OR HOW ABOUT A 5-FOOT-LONG SECTIONAL PHOTOMURAL? BEST of ALL, THIS UNIT IS HIGHLY NOMADIC: TAKEN APART IT IS → 2 FRAMES, 2 LEGS, 8 SCREWS + INSETS.

ORIGINAL VERSION

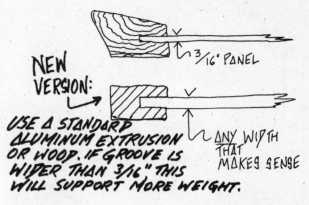

NEW VERSION: →

3/16" PANEL

USE A STANDARD ALUMINUM EXTRUSION OR WOOD. IF GROOVE IS WIDER THAN 3/16" THIS WILL SUPPORT MORE WEIGHT.

ANY WIDTH THAT MAKES SENSE

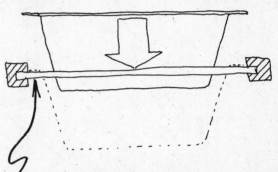

WOODEN OR MASONITE SQUARE TO SLIDE IN & CUT OUT SO RECORD PLAYER OR PLASTIC TRAY CAN DROP IN.

NO SCREWS OTHER THAN THE 8 AND NO GLUE ARE NEEDED.

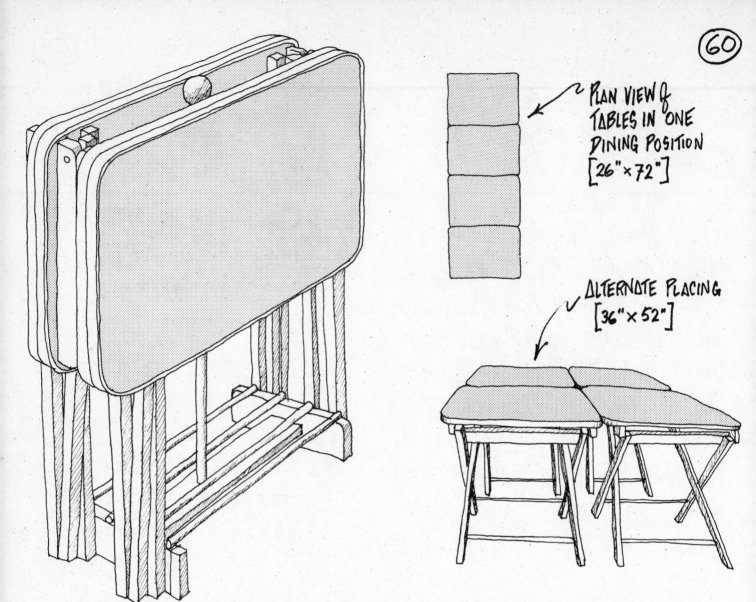

PLAN VIEW OF
TABLES IN ONE
DINING POSITION
[26" × 72"]

ALTERNATE PLACING
[36" × 52"]

NEARLY ALL FURNITURE & DEPARTMENT STORES SELL SETS OF FOUR FOLDING TABLES. THESE MAKE GREAT SENSE, STANDING NEXT TO INDIVIDUAL CHAIRS FOR SUPPER. WE HAVE INCREASED ALL DIMENSIONS, SO THAT THE TABLES NOW STAND 26 INCHES TALL, WHICH MAKES THEM PERFECT NEXT TO A CHAIR, BUT ALSO PERMITS FOUR, SIX, OR EIGHT OF THEM TO FASTEN TOGETHER INTO A SOMEWHAT LOWER-THAN-AVERAGE DINING TABLE, SEATING 6 TO 10 PEOPLE. TABLE-TOPS ARE NOW 26" × 18". FOR THE BUILDING YOU CAN COPY THE JUNKY PLASTIC & METAL SETS NOW AVAILABLE. IF YOU BUILD YOUR OWN OF HARDWOOD LEGS & PLY-TOPS AND TO OUR SIZES, PROVIDE A LIP OR OVERHANG TO THE TOPS. THIS WILL PERMIT YOU TO JOIN THEM INTO A DINING-TABLE WITH SMALL "C"-CLAMPS.

## Simple Drawing Table:

IF YOU LIKE TO DO DRAWING, DRAUGHTING, LAYOUT or PASTE-UP WORK IN A STANDING POSITION, THEN THIS IS ONE of THE SIMPLEST NOMADIC SOLUTIONS TO YOUR PROBLEMS. BY BEING A WALL~HUNG UNIT, IT FREES TABLE SURFACES, ESSENTIAL WHEN ROOMS ARE SMALL & SPACE IS VALUABLE.

JIM & VIC BOTH PREFER TO DRAW STANDING UP, FEELING THAT THIS LEADS TO NEATER WORK.

VIC BUILT THIS SYSTEM WHILE WORKING OUT of A SMALL HUT IN BALI. BASICALLY THERE ARE JUST TWO METAL [WROUGHT IRON] STRAPS, BENT INTO THE TRIANGULAR WALL BRACKETS. THESE ARE SCRIBED TO WALL STUDS, ABOUT 6"-9" IN FROM THE TWO SIDE EDGES of THE BOARD. TWO WOODSCREWS PER BRACKET HOLD THE BOARD IN PLACE. YOU MAY USE AN EXISTING DRAWING BOARD, 3/4" PLYWOOD or CHIP~BOARD. A PARALLEL RULER CAN BE INSTALLED. PLACE AT COMFORTABLE WORKING HEIGHT.

$\frac{1}{4}$" WROUGHT IRON STRAP, 2" WIDE, MAKE ②

WALL

36"-45" FROM FLOOR, DEPENDING ON YOUR HEIGHT

FLOOR

# Hex Tables:

AS A WHOLE SERIES OF VERY LOW TABLES, HEXAGONAL TOPS ARE USEFUL. LIKE THE CELLS IN A BEE'S HONEYCOMB, THEY FIT TOGETHER WITHOUT WASTE.

THIS SET OF SIX TABLES PLUS ONE PLANTER & 4 HAND-WOVEN HEX CUSHIONS, WAS DESIGNED & BUILT BY VIC SOME YEARS AGO. THEY ARE TWO LEVELS TALL. THE MAJORITY [PLANTER, 2 WALNUT-PLYWOOD-TOPPED ONES, THE ONE WITH HEXAGONAL TILES INSET INTO THE TOP & WALNUT EDGED, AND THE MARBLE-TOPPED TABLE] ARE 12" HIGH. THE TWO WORMY CHESTNUT TOPS ARE 9" HIGH. THE CUSHIONS ARE EACH 3" THICK. VERTICAL LEG SUPPORTS ARE PAINTED FLAT BLACK.

THIS TOTAL UNIT SERVES BOTH AS "COFFEE TABLE" AS WELL AS A "DINING TABLE" FOR INFORMAL SUPPERS. CHAIRS USED WITH IT ARE DIRECTORS CHAIRS, BEANBAGS OR JUST RECLINING DIRECTLY ON THE CARPET. FOR EXTRA COMPANY, SOME OF THE CUSHIONS CAN BE LAID ON TABLES → PRESTO: AN UPHOLSTERED STOOL! THESE TABLES STAND ABUSE WELL & ARE HIGHLY NOMADIC: THEY'VE BEEN IN HARD USE 12 YEARS AND MOVED 17 TIMES. BEST OF ALL: VIC BUILT EACH TABLE IN 30 MINUTES!

# How to Draw a Hexagon:

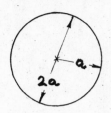

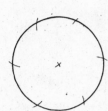

1. DECIDE ON THE SIZE YOU WANT & SET COMPASS TO THE LENGTH OF THE SIDE OF HEXAGON (a). THIS WILL BE THE RADIUS OF THE CIRCLE & ALSO ½ THE CIRCLE'S DIAMETER. DRAW CIRCLE.

2. WITH THE COMPASS STILL SET TO THE RADIUS (a), MARK OFF THIS RADIUS 6 TIMES AROUND THE CIRCLE'S EDGE.

3. CONNECT THE 6 POINTS YOU HAVE MARKED OFF WITH STRAIGHT LINES. YOU NOW HAVE A HEXAGON, ALL OF ITS SIDES ARE (a) IN LENGTH.

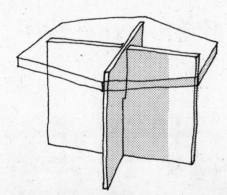

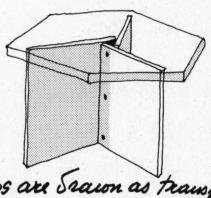

JIM HAS DRAWN SOME VARIATIONS ON HEX TABLE SUPPORTS [Note: tops are drawn as transparent].

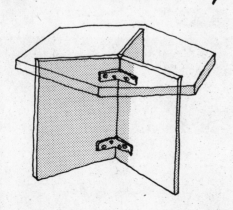

YOU CAN VARY SIZES & MATERIALS AS YOU SEE FIT.

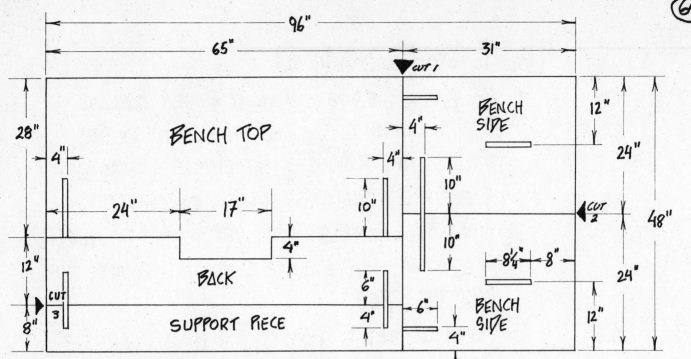

96"

65"    31"

CUT 1

28"

BENCH TOP

4"    4"

BENCH SIDE

12"

24"

4"    4"

10"

24"

24"    17"

10"

10"

10"

CUT 2

48"

12"

4"

BACK

6"    8¼"    8"

8"

CUT 3

SUPPORT PIECE

6"    6"

4"

BENCH SIDE

24"

4"

12"

Note: ALL SLOTS ARE SLIGHTLY WIDER THAN ¾". ALLOW 1/16" WIDER STILL, IF YOU PLAN TO PAINT THE SURFACES.

JIM'S WORK BENCH & DESK IS MADE OF ONE SHEET OF STANDARD ¾" PLYWOOD. YOU MAY SUBSTITUTE CHIP-BOARD FOR THIS. IN THE PHOTO, DON'T BE CONFUSED BY THE STOOL IN THE MIDDLE. [BY THE WAY, ALL THE SMALL PARTS ARE IN BABY-FOOD JARS, ATTACHED TO PERFORATED MASONITE WITH CLEVER PLASTIC LIDS. → THEY ARE CALLED "HANDY DANDY" AND ARE AVAILABLE FROM → WICKLIFFE INDUSTRIES, BOX 286-MX-12, WICKLIFFE, OHIO, USA.

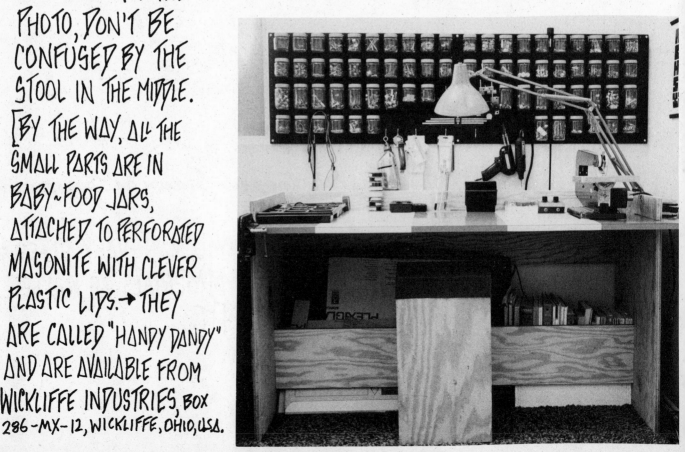

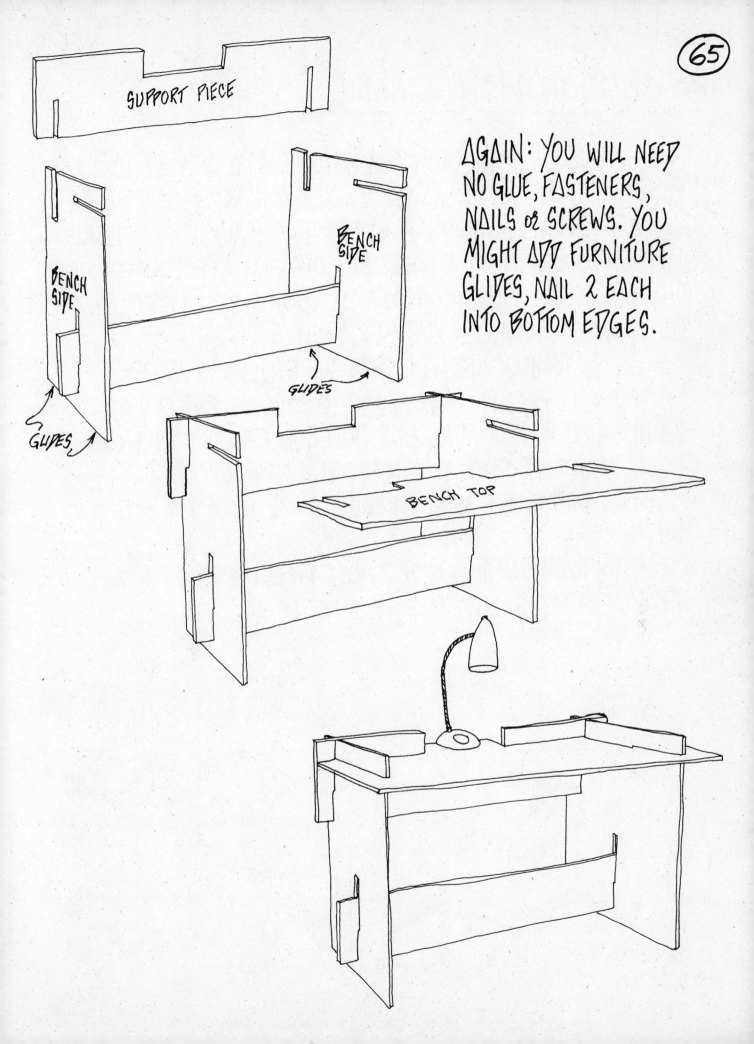

SUPPORT PIECE

BENCH SIDE

BENCH SIDE

GLIDES

GLIDES

BENCH TOP

AGAIN: YOU WILL NEED NO GLUE, FASTENERS, NAILS OR SCREWS. YOU MIGHT ADD FURNITURE GLIDES, NAIL 2 EACH INTO BOTTOM EDGES.

# 4~Position Drawing Table:

Working at the California Institute of the Arts, we use drawing tables that were specifically designed & custom~built. They are over~dimensioned, incredibly heavy, noisy, nearly impossible to adjust, imprecise, tops fall off. Furthermore they are dangerous, institutional looking, grotesquely ugly, badly finished & very expensive....

Naturally we felt that we could develop a better & less expensive Four~positional table that would also be nomadic. Our question really was: how long would it take to find such a new concept?

This table is the result of 2½ hours of intensive work.

Caution: This is the most difficult piece in the book → Don't undertake it first!

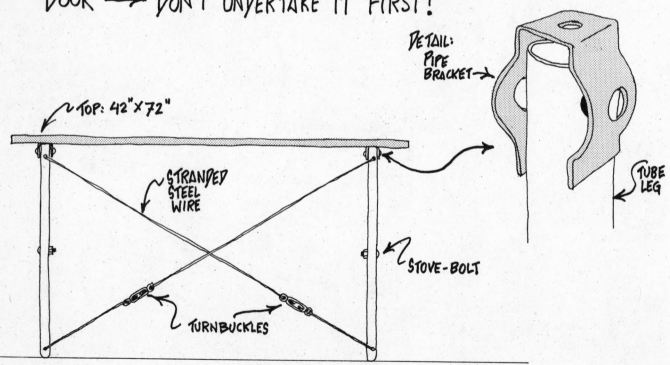

TOP: 42" X 72"

DETAIL:
PIPE
BRACKET →

STRANDED
STEEL
WIRE

STOVE-BOLT

TUBE
LEG

TURNBUCKLES

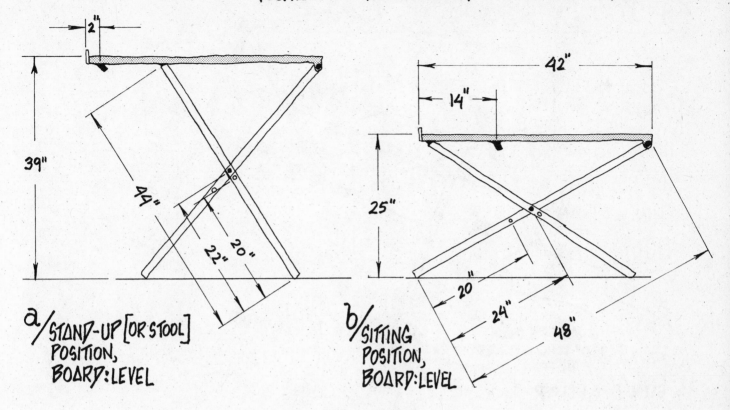

2"

39"

44"

20"

22"

a/ STAND-UP [OR STOOL] POSITION, BOARD: LEVEL

42"

14"

25"

20

24"

48"

b/ SITTING POSITION, BOARD: LEVEL

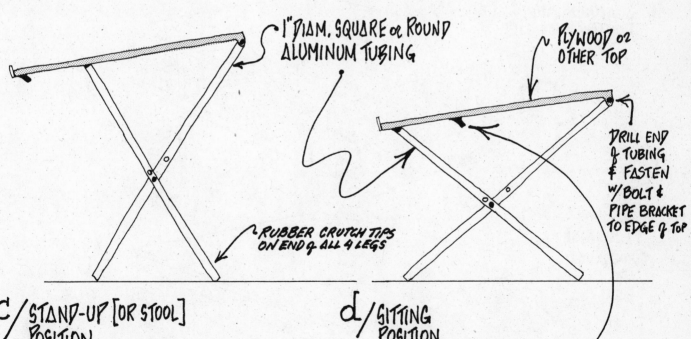

1" DIAM. SQUARE or ROUND ALUMINUM TUBING

PLYWOOD or OTHER TOP

DRILL END of TUBING & FASTEN w/ BOLT & PIPE BRACKET TO EDGE of TOP

RUBBER CRUTCH TIPS ON END of ALL 4 LEGS

c/ STAND-UP [OR STOOL] POSITION, BOARD: INCLINED

d/ SITTING POSITION, BOARD: INCLINED

Note: TO CHANGE TABLE FROM HIGH TO LOW, MOVE LEGS OF STRUCTURE.
TO CHANGE FROM LEVEL TO INCLINED CHANGE PIVOT POINTS WHICH ARE 2 STOVE BOLTS.

FOR LEG RETAINER STOPS: BUY 3/4" WOOD DOWEL & CUT OFF 4 PIECES, EA. ABOUT 2" LONG. GLUE THESE INTO 4 PIECES of 3/4" PLYWOOD, EA. 2"×2" WHICH ARE FASTENED TO UNDERSIDE of TABLE-TOP.

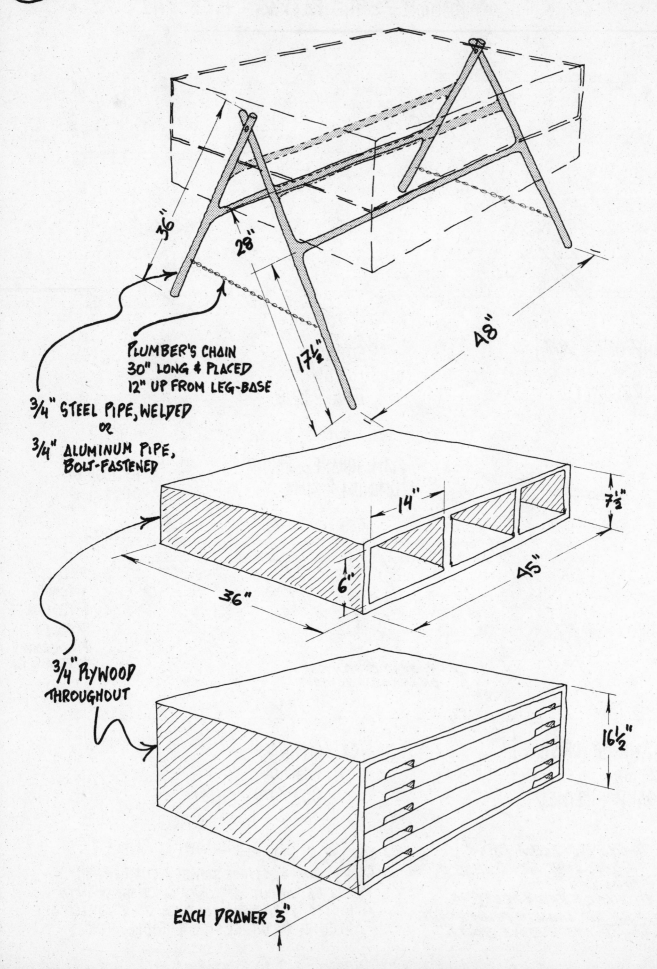

PLUMBER'S CHAIN
30" LONG & PLACED
12" UP FROM LEG-BASE

3/4" STEEL PIPE, WELDED
OR
3/4" ALUMINUM PIPE,
BOLT-FASTENED

36"

28"

17½"

48"

14"

7½"

6"

45"

36"

3/4" PLYWOOD
THROUGHOUT

16½"

EACH DRAWER 3"

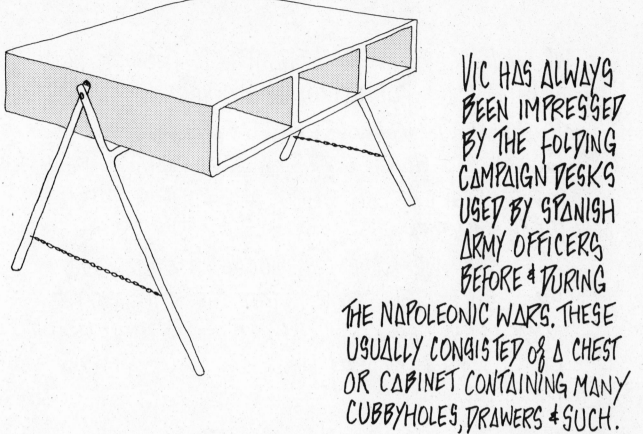

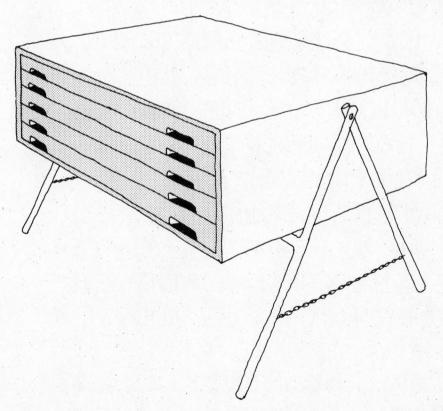

VIC HAS ALWAYS BEEN IMPRESSED BY THE FOLDING CAMPAIGN DESKS USED BY SPANISH ARMY OFFICERS BEFORE & DURING THE NAPOLEONIC WARS. THESE USUALLY CONSISTED OF A CHEST OR CABINET CONTAINING MANY CUBBYHOLES, DRAWERS & SUCH. THE SECOND PART WOULD BE FOLDING LEG~STRUCTURES INTO WHICH THE CHEST PART COULD BE SET FOR USE IN THE FIELD.

HERE ARE OUR TWO VERSIONS: ONE IS A DESK, THE OTHER A GENEROUS STORAGE CABINET FOR DRAWINGS, PRINTS & ARTWORK.

WE HAVE MADE EVERY ATTEMPT TO PROVIDE YOU WITH BASIC INFORMATION IN THIS SECTION. IN ORDER TO BUILD DINING & WORKING TABLES WE HAVE GIVEN YOU BASIC SIZES, A GREAT MANY IDEAS FOR SUPPORT OR LEG UNITS, AND SOME MATERIAL IDEAS FOR TOPS.

WE HAVE CONSCIOUSLY STAYED AWAY FROM SUCH WELL-KNOWN STRUCTURES AS A TABLE MADE FROM CABLE REEL SPOOLS, OR A CABLE REEL END [WHICH IS ROUND], NAILED TO A BARREL FOR ITS SUPPORT.

BUT WE HAVE ALSO CAREFULLY LEFT OUT SUCH EXOTICA AS ROUND, JAPANESE HIBACHI COOKERS INSTALLED IN TABLE TOPS, MARBLE SURFACING, CORK CUSHIONING UNDER TYPEWRITERS, ILLUMINATED TRACING TOPS ON DRAWING TABLES, SOLID BRASS PIANO HINGES, AND MUCH ELSE.

AGAIN LET US REMIND YOU THAT ALL WE HAVE GIVEN YOU ARE STARTERS. FEEL FREE TO CHANGE, ADAPT, REDESIGN OR IMPROVE ON ANYTHING YOU'VE FOUND IN THIS SECTION OR, FOR THAT MATTER, THE WHOLE BOOK.

IF YOU THINK UP BETTER WAYS, DO AS, WE HAVE DONE ➤ SHARE THEM WITH OTHERS!

# STORAGE:

THE SIMPLEST WAY TO CUT DOWN ON STORAGE IS TO OWN LESS. THIS IS NOT SAID FACETIOUSLY. LIVING IN A SOCIETY THAT HAS TAUGHT "COMPETENT CONSUMERISM" TO ITS YOUNG FOR MANY DECADES, A SOCIETY IN WHICH MANY ATTEMPT TO ASSERT THEIR OWN PERSONALITIES THROUGH OWNING GLITTERING STATUS OBJECTS, DOING MORE WITH LESS IS APT TO BE DIFFICULT.

BUT EVEN FROM THE SIMPLE VIEWPOINT OF ECOLOGY, WE MUST ALL LOOK AT WHAT WE OWN AND ASK OURSELVES → CAN I DO WITHOUT IT? DO I NEED TO REPLACE IT? CAN I DO WITH LESS?

FROM A NOMADIC VIEW, THE LESS WE OWN, THE LESS WE HAVE TO MOVE.

IN RE-EVALUATING THEIR POSSESSIONS, VIC & HARLANNE FOUND THAT NEARLY EVERYTHING COULD BE DIVIDED INTO THREE PILES:

FIRST THOSE THINGS THAT "ONE CANNOT LIVE WITHOUT": CLOTHING, BEDDING, DISHES : OF COURSE. BUT OTHER THINGS FILL REAL NEEDS TOO: BOOKS,

PHONOGRAPH RECORDS, TAPES, CERAMICS, PAINTINGS, FLOWERS, PRINTS, WOVEN HANGINGS, WHAT-HAVE-YOU. THESE BITS OF INFORMATION [AS IN BOOKS or RECORDINGS], or THESE HANDCRAFTED OBJECTS [REPRESENTING LOVE], or THE FLOWERS & PLANTS [CELEBRATING LIFE] FILL DEEP HUMAN NEEDS. ALSO ESSENTIAL ARE TOOLS, CAMERA, ETC.

THE SECOND PILE CONSISTS of THINGS WE CAN DO WITHOUT — EASILY: THAT GORPY LAMP, ELECTRIC COOKIE DEHUMIDIFIER, THE 7 or 8 CLOCKS [WHEN ONE IS PLENTY], THE CARVING SET USED EVERY YEAR or SO. ALSO THOSE THINGS WE ONLY THINK WE NEED: DO WE NEED A WELL-APPOINTED DARKROOM, WHEN THERE ARE BETTER ONES AT THE YMCA, THE LOCAL COLLEGE & EVERY OTHER CHURCH BASEMENT? MUST WE MAKE MONTHLY PAYMENTS ON A SLOWLY DETERIORATING WASHER/DRYER WITH A 25¢ LAUNDERETTE AROUND THE CORNER?

FINALLY THERE ARE THOSE THINGS OVER WHICH WE HAVE "CUSTODIAL CARE". GRANDMOTHER'S GRANDFATHER CLOCK, A CHAIR BY FRANK LLOYD WRIGHT, UNCLE THEOBALD'S FAVOURITE EASY-CHAIR. ON THIS LAST CATEGORY WE CANNOT ADVISE YOU. AS FOR OURSELVES: ITS ALL IN "DEAD STORAGE".

IF BY NOW YOU'VE GONE THROUGH THIS RE-EVALUATION, READ ON: YOU'RE READY TO STORE WHAT YOU REALLY NEED.

ORANGE CRATES ARE STILL ONE OF THE SIMPLEST WAYS TO STORE
BOOKS, RECORDS, DISHES, ROLLED-UP SWEATERS OR WHAT-HAVE-YOU.
WE HAVE CHOSEN THIS PARTICULAR ILLUSTRATION, BECAUSE IT
SHOWS AN ENTIRE BOOKSTORE BUILT OF FRUIT-CRATES. THIS WAS
BUILT BY STUDENTS IN MILANO LAST YEAR, TO SELL USED TEXT-BOOKS,
RARE BOOKS AND ASSOCIATED ITEMS.
THE BASES ARE FORMED BY FLAT GRAPE BOXES, THE ACTUAL
BOOK STORAGE BY ORANGE CRATES. THESE ALSO FORM THE WALLS
OF THE BUILDING, WITH SHEETS OF MYLAR AS A ROOF.
→ BY LOOKING CAREFULLY YOU CAN BUY USED SODA CRATES IN (73)
THE FAMILY-SIZE BOTTLES. THESE ARE WOOD & STEEL-REINFORCED.

3"
3"
3"
3"

## "SIMPLEST" BOOK CASE:

THIS PARTICULAR BOOKCASE IS VERY POPULAR IN SWEDEN. IT IS MADE OF 3/4" PARTICLE BOARD OR CHIPBOARD. AS YOU CAN SEE ON THE NEXT PAGE, IT CAN ALSO BE CUT OUT OF A SINGLE SHEET OF BOARD OR PLYWOOD.

SINCE IT IS BOTH EASY TO MAKE & INEXPENSIVE, WE'LL TRY TO GIVE YOU EXACT IN~ STRUCTIONS:

1/ CUT OUT THE TWO UPRIGHTS, THE TEN SHELVES AND THE TWO 3" SPACERS.

2/ SCREW ONE 3" SPACER TO TOP SHELF, 6 INCHES FROM FRONT EDGE OF SHELF. SCREW THE OTHER 3" SPACER TO BOTTOM SHELF, 3 INCHES FROM FRONT EDGE OF SHELF.

3/ NOW SCREW THE TOP AND BOTTOM SHELVES WITH ATTACHED SPACERS TO THE TWO UP~ RIGHTS [USING #8 2½" FLATHEAD WOODSCREWS] BEING CAREFUL TO ATTACH BOTH SHELVES & SPACERS TO UPRIGHTS WITH SCREWS.

4/ DRILL HOLES IN UPRIGHTS WHEREVER YOU WISH TO LOCATE THE OTHER EIGHT SHELVES.

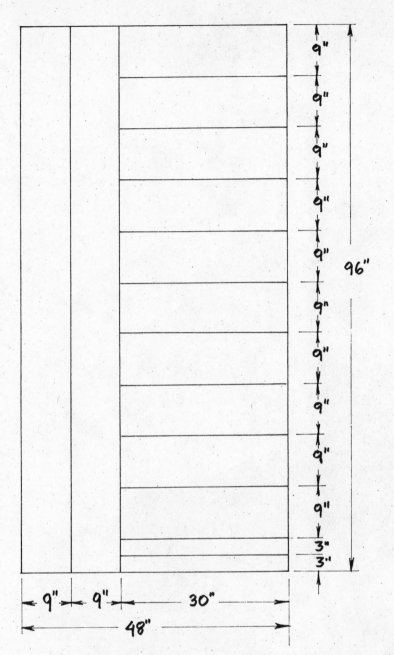

9"
9"
9"
9"
9"
9"
9"
9"
9"
9"
3"
3"

96"

9" | 9" | 30"
48"

5/ ATTACH SHELVES WITH SCREWS.

## VARIATIONS:

- SINCE THE BOOKCASE HAS NO BACK, THE TWO 3" SPACERS ARE ALL THAT PROVIDES STURDINESS UNTIL SHELVES & LOAD ARE APPLIED → SO YOU MAY GLUE AND USE SCREWS, BUT REMEMBER → THE PIECE IS NOW LESS NOMADIC.

- YOU CAN MAKE IT LOWER [84" IS A GOOD HEIGHT] & USE FEWER SHELVES.

- IF YOU BUILD TWO, YOU HAVE REALLY BUILT THREE: PLACE THE TWO YOU'VE BUILT 30 INCHES APART & INSTALL MORE SHELVES BETWEEN THEM.

- THIS STEEL SHELF SUPPORT IS CHEAP AND AVAILABLE AT ALL HARDWARE STORES. TO USE IT, SIMPLY DRILL HOLE ON INSIDES & UPRIGHTS & LAY THE SHELVES IN. THAT MAKES YOUR SHELVES ADJUSTABLE, DEPENDING ONLY ON HOW MANY HOLES YOU'VE DRILLED. IT TAKES 4 SUPPORTS PER SHELF.

PHOTO BY: TIM STREET-PORTER from "DESIGN" [ENGLAND], ISSUE № 242

THE BRITISH ARCHITECTS FARRELL/GRIMSHAW DEVELOPED THIS "TROLLEY FURNITURE PACKAGE" FOR A STUDENT HOSTEL. THE KIT CONSISTS OF: A BED ON CASTORS WHICH FITS UNDER THE MAIN FRAME, WHICH IS ALSO ON CASTORS; A CHAIR, LAMP, PLASTIC DRAWERS, ADJUSTABLE SHELVING, ADJUSTABLE DESK TOP, WASTE-BIN, COFFEE TABLE, CLOTHES CLOSET WITH MIRRORED DOOR CONTAINING SMALL SHELVING, ETC.. PACKAGE SELLS
FOR £72.- IN ENGLAND. YOU MIGHT USE YOUR OWN INGENUITY IN DE~

VELOPING SOME EVEN MORE NOMADIC, KNOCK~DOWN "LIVING CUBE". THE GREAT ADVANTAGE of HAVING THIS KIND of PORTABLE ENVIRONMENT IS, THAT YOU ARE THEN ABLE TO COMPLETELY DISREGARD THE <u>REAL</u> APARTMENT AND ITS SHABBYNESS, INTO WHICH YOU THEN INSTALL YOUR "LIVING CUBE", AND USE ONLY THOSE LIFE~SUPPORT FUNCTIONS INHERENT IN THE APARTMENT WHICH YOUR CUBE DOES NOT HAVE:

- OUTLETS FOR LIGHTING, TELEPHONE & TV-JACKS
- RUNNING HOT & COLD WATER, SINKS, SHOWER & TUB
- HEATING SYSTEM
- REFRIGERATOR
- CLOSETS & FLOORING → TO STOW THINGS
- A ROOF TO KEEP AWAY RAIN
- WALLS FOR INSULATION
- A MAIL-BOX FOR COMMUNICATION

BY THUS <u>DISREGARDING</u> THE VARIOUS REAL APARTMENT INTERIORS THROUGH WHICH YOU MOVE WITH YOUR "LIVING CUBE" OVER THE YEARS YOU ARE ALSO MAKING SURE THAT ALL YOUR INVESTMENTS IN MONEY, MATERIALS, TIME & LABOUR ARE CONFINED TO THAT WHICH YOU OWN & MOVE. SINCE YOU ARE IN FACT DEVELOPING A SORT of "INDOOR TENT" YOU CAN CREATE WALLS & SPACE DIVIDERS WITHIN THE UNIT OUT of THE MOST FRAGILE MATERIALS: PAPER, FABRIC, ETC.

(SEE ALSO VIC'S BOOK "<u>DESIGN FOR THE REAL WORLD</u>", N.Y., PANTHEON BOOKS, 1972, PAGES 116 -117.)

ON THE FOLLOWING PAGES WE SHOW A FEW POSSIBLE CUBES.

# ENTERTAINING CUBE:

THIS WHOLE SERIES OF CUBES IS CONSTRUCTED OF 2"×2" DOUGLAS FIR or PINE AND ¾" PLYWOOD PANELS, PLUS ROPE, FABRICS, DOWELS, ETC. ALL THE CUBES ARE 8×8×8 FEET.

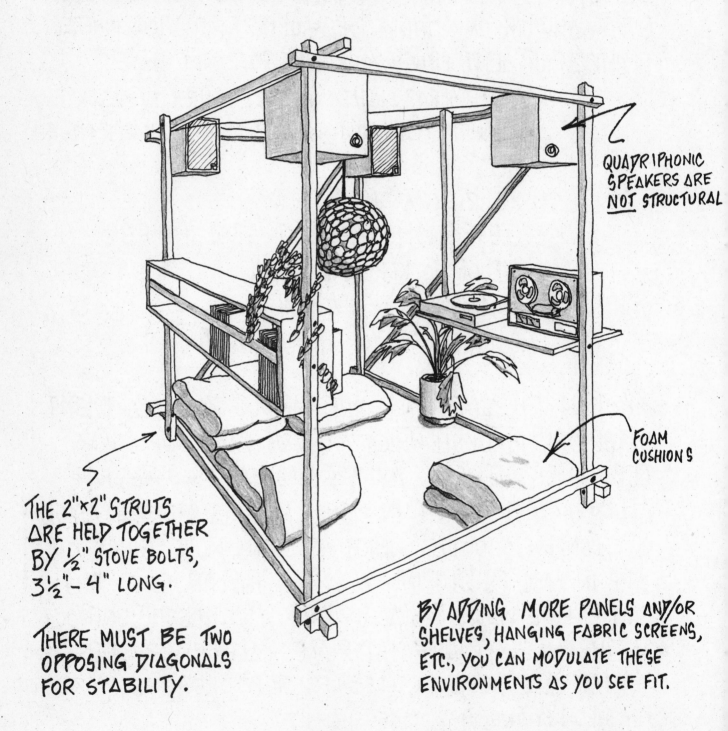

QUADRIPHONIC SPEAKERS ARE NOT STRUCTURAL

FOAM CUSHIONS

THE 2"×2" STRUTS ARE HELD TOGETHER BY ½" STOVE BOLTS, 3½"-4" LONG.

THERE MUST BE TWO OPPOSING DIAGONALS FOR STABILITY.

BY ADDING MORE PANELS and/or SHELVES, HANGING FABRIC SCREENS, ETC., YOU CAN MODULATE THESE ENVIRONMENTS AS YOU SEE FIT.

note: FOR BUBBLE LAMP, SEE PAGE 111

# CHILDREN'S CUBE:

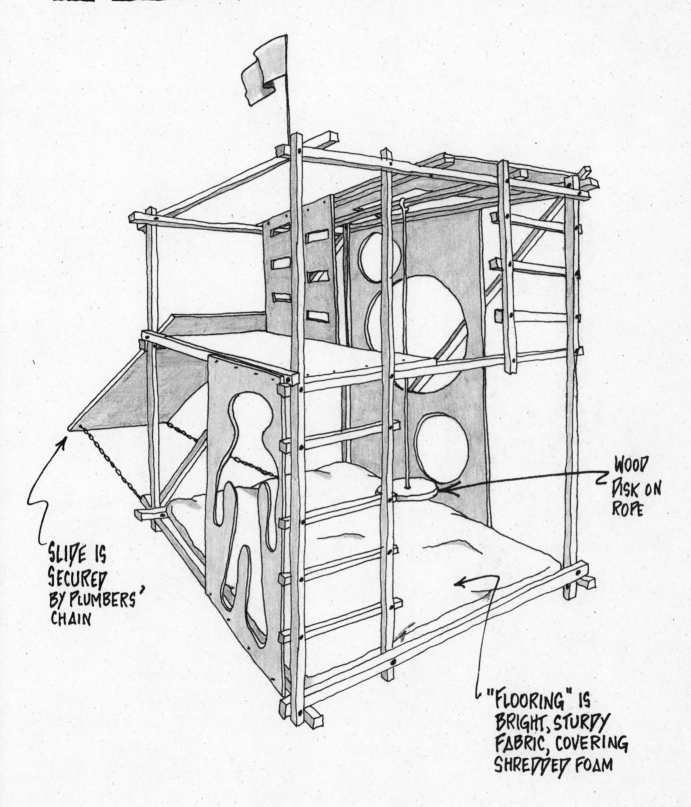

SLIDE IS
SECURED
BY PLUMBERS'
CHAIN

WOOD
DISK ON
ROPE

"FLOORING" IS
BRIGHT, STURDY
FABRIC, COVERING
SHREDDED FOAM

# RELAXATION CUBE:

80

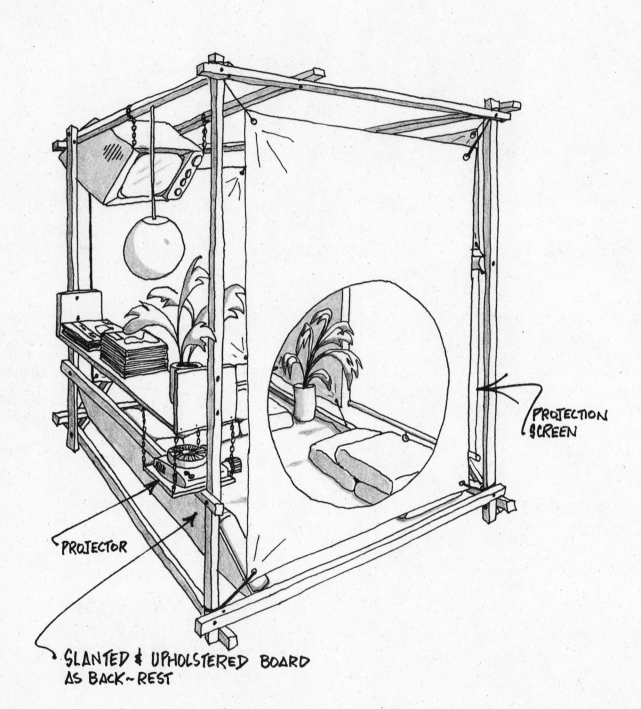

PROJECTION SCREEN

PROJECTOR

SLANTED & UPHOLSTERED BOARD
AS BACK~REST

# WORK CUBE:

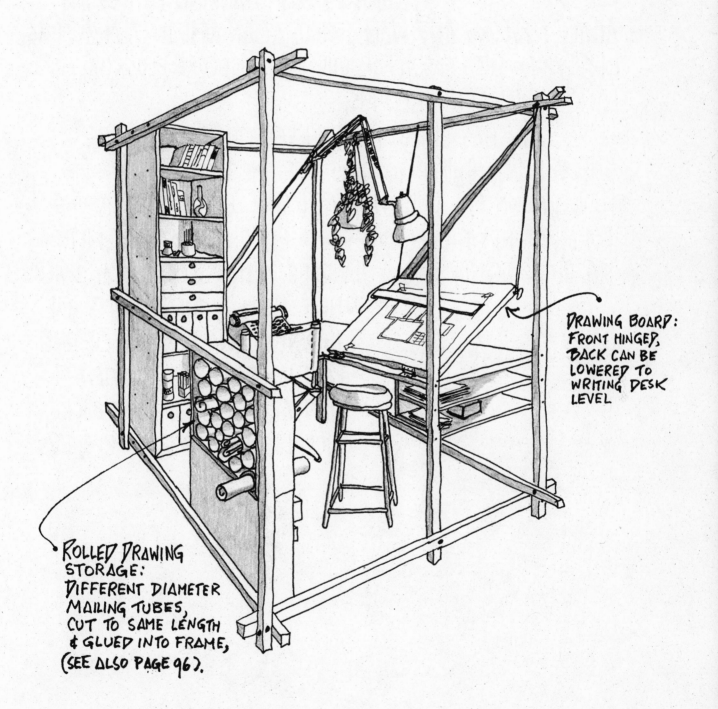

DRAWING BOARD:
FRONT HINGED,
BACK CAN BE
LOWERED TO
WRITING DESK
LEVEL

ROLLED DRAWING
STORAGE:
DIFFERENT DIAMETER
MAILING TUBES,
CUT TO SAME LENGTH
& GLUED INTO FRAME,
(SEE ALSO PAGE 96).

# A COMBINATION of PACKING CRATES FOR BOOKS PLUS SUPPORT:

VIC ORIGINALLY DEVELOPED THIS NEW SUPPORT CONCEPT FOR BOOK~SHELVING, WHICH IS SELF~STANDING BY RESTING AGAINST FLOORS AND WALL, WHILE AT AN ASSUAN DAM MEETING IN EGYPT. THE REASON FOR THIS WAS INSECURE FLOORING AND LACK of AVAILABLE SHELVING.

JIM HAS SINCE THEN DEVELOPED THE "HANGING" SHELVES INTO SHIPPING BOXES FOR THE BOOKS. BELOW WE HAVE DRAWN ONE UNIT WITH FIVE SHELVES IN PLACE, IN THE FOREGROUND THE BOTTOM SHELF FOR THE NEXT UNIT WITH ITS SHIPPING TOP & ROPE HANDLES. NATURALLY YOU CAN BUILD A WHOLE WALL of THESE UNITS. IN THE NEXT TWO PAGES of CUTTING DIAGRAMS, WE HAVE ASSUMED STANDARD SIZES FOR PAPERBACKS, NOVELS, ART BOOKS, RECORDS, ETC.

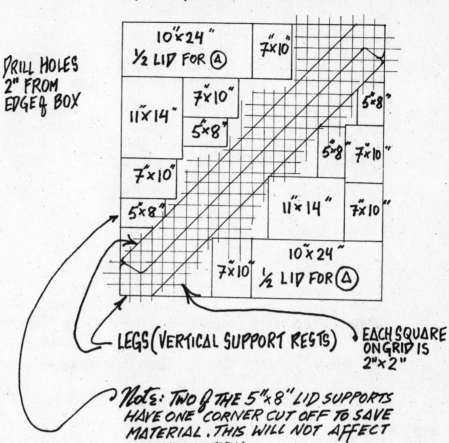

2 Ⓒ BOXES

DRILL HOLES 2" FROM EDGE OF BOX

2 Ⓐ BOXES

1 BOX Ⓑ

10"×24" ½ LID FOR Ⓐ

7"×10"

11"×14"

7"×10"

5"×8"

5"×8"

7"×10"

5"×8"

5"×8"

7"×10"

11"×14"

7"×10"

5"×8"

7"×10"

10"×24" ½ LID FOR Ⓐ

LEGS (VERTICAL SUPPORT RESTS)

EACH SQUARE ON GRID IS 2"×2"

YOU CAN USE THIS SIDE VIEW AS A LAYOUT PLAN. UNIT RESTS AGAINST WALL & FLOOR. BOXES ARE MOUNTED BY ADEQUATE-SIZED STOVE BOLTS OR "T" NUTS (SEE PAGE 89). THESE BOLTS OR NUTS ARE REMOVED & ROPE HANDLES INSERTED WHEN MOVING.

Note: TWO OF THE 5"×8" LID SUPPORTS HAVE ONE CORNER CUT OFF TO SAVE MATERIAL. THIS WILL NOT AFFECT CONSTRUCTION.

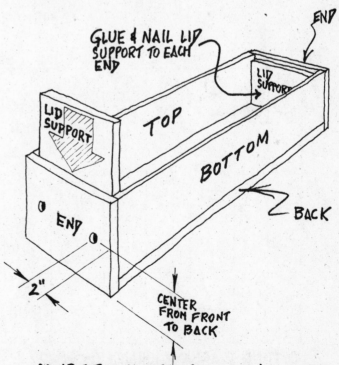

GLUE & NAIL LID SUPPORT TO EACH END

END

LID SUPPORT

LID SUPPORT

TOP

BOTTOM

BACK

END

2"

CENTER FROM FRONT TO BACK

SAMPLE BOX CONSTRUCTION: NAIL & GLUE BOX TOGETHER, THEN DRILL MOUNTING HOLES 2 INCHES IN FROM TOP & BOTTOM & CENTERED FROM FRONT TO BACK.

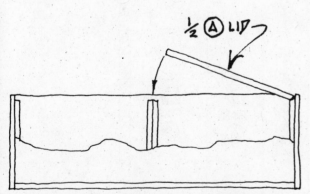

½ Ⓐ LID

ONE OF THE 2 Ⓐ BOXES HAS A 2-PART LID. NAIL & GLUE THE 2 EXTRA 7"×10" LID SUPPORTS IN CENTER OF BOX AS SHOWN

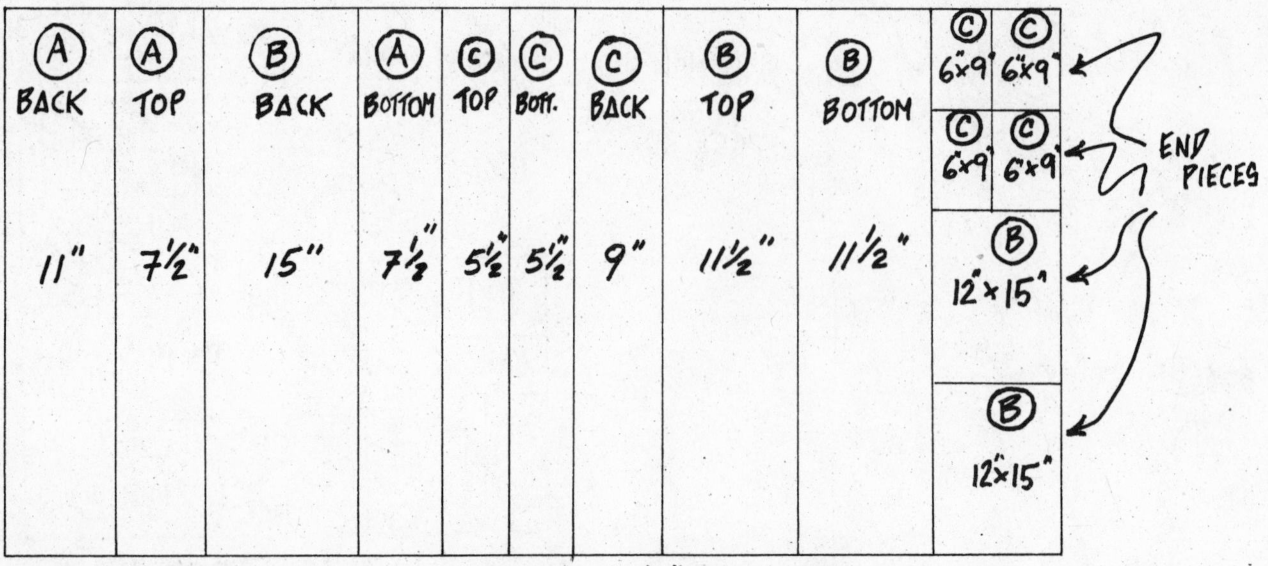

Top diagram, left to right columns:

| (A) BACK | (A) TOP | (B) BACK | (A) BOTTOM | (C) TOP | (C) BOT. | (C) BACK | (B) TOP | (B) BOTTOM |
|---|---|---|---|---|---|---|---|---|
| 11" | 7½" | 15" | 7½" | 5½" | 5½" | 9" | 11½" | 11½" |

Right column pieces:
- (C) 6"x9"   (C) 6"x9"
- (C) 6"x9"   (C) 6"x9"
- (B) 12"x15"
- (B) 12"x15"

→ END PIECES

**CUTTING DIAGRAM : 1 SHEET 4×8-FOOT ½" PLYWOOD**

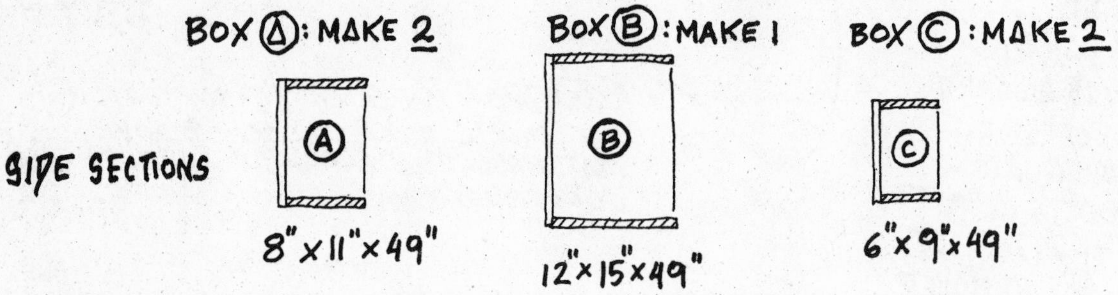

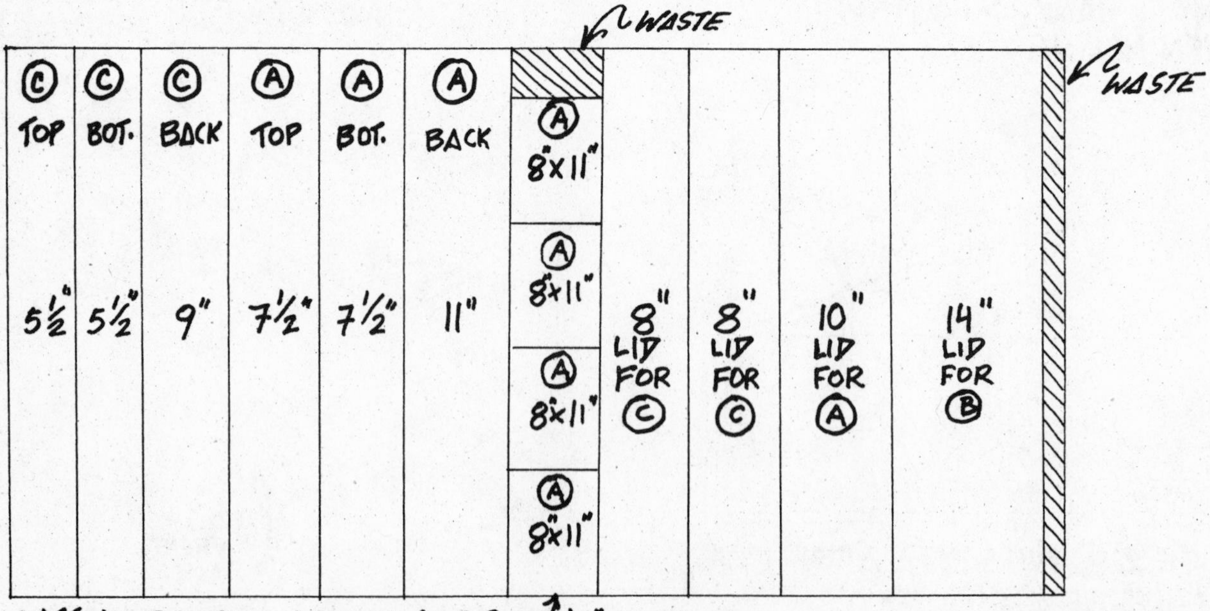

BOX (A): MAKE 2    BOX (B): MAKE 1    BOX (C): MAKE 2

SIDE SECTIONS

(A) 8"×11"×49"    (B) 12"×15"×49"    (C) 6"×9"×49"

Bottom diagram:

WASTE

| (C) TOP | (C) BOT. | (C) BACK | (A) TOP | (A) BOT. | (A) BACK |
|---|---|---|---|---|---|
| 5½" | 5½" | 9" | 7½" | 7½" | 11" |

Center pieces:
- (A) 8"×11"
- (A) 8"×11"
- (A) 8"×11"
- (A) 8"×11"

Right columns:
- 8" LID FOR (C)
- 8" LID FOR (C)
- 10" LID FOR (A)
- 14" LID FOR (B)

WASTE

**CUTTING DIAGRAM: 1 SHEET 4×8-FOOT ½" PLYWOOD**

END PIECES

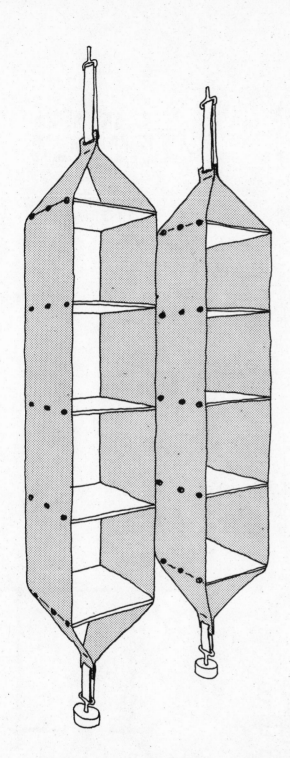

THESE SUSPENDED BOOK-SHELVES OF HEMP CANVAS WERE DESIGNED BY JØRGEN HØI OF DENMARK. THE INSET SHELVES ARE MADE OF ALUMINUM & THE WHOLE UNIT COLLAPSES FOR MOVING. WEIGHTS ON THE BOTTOM KEEP THE UNIT FROM TURNING.

→ AVAILABLE from:
DEN PERMANENTE,
VESTERPORT,
COPENHAGEN V, DENMARK

→ THE UNITS ARE SURPRISINGLY STRONG & WE FEEL THAT YOU CAN MAKE YOUR OWN VARIATIONS. TO DO THAT, WE SUGGEST YOU USE ½" PLYWOOD SHELVES, PUT BRASS GROMMETS THROUGH THE CANVAS & USE WOODSCREWS TO SECURE THEM.

NOTICE THAT BESIDES BOOKS, EVEN A SMALL TV-SET IS SUPPORTED AS THE PICTURE TO THE RIGHT SHOWS. A GOOD IDEA SOON SPREADS. THE UNITS ARE NOW MADE OF FIBREGLASS-REINFORCED HEAVY PAPER, COME IN WHITE, YELLOW, ORANGE, RED, BLUE & BLACK & ARE 2 METERS (78") TALL. PULLIRSCH + WEBER OF MUNICH, GERMANY ARE THE RIP-OFF ARTISTS RESPONSIBLE. (COURTESY: "FORM".)

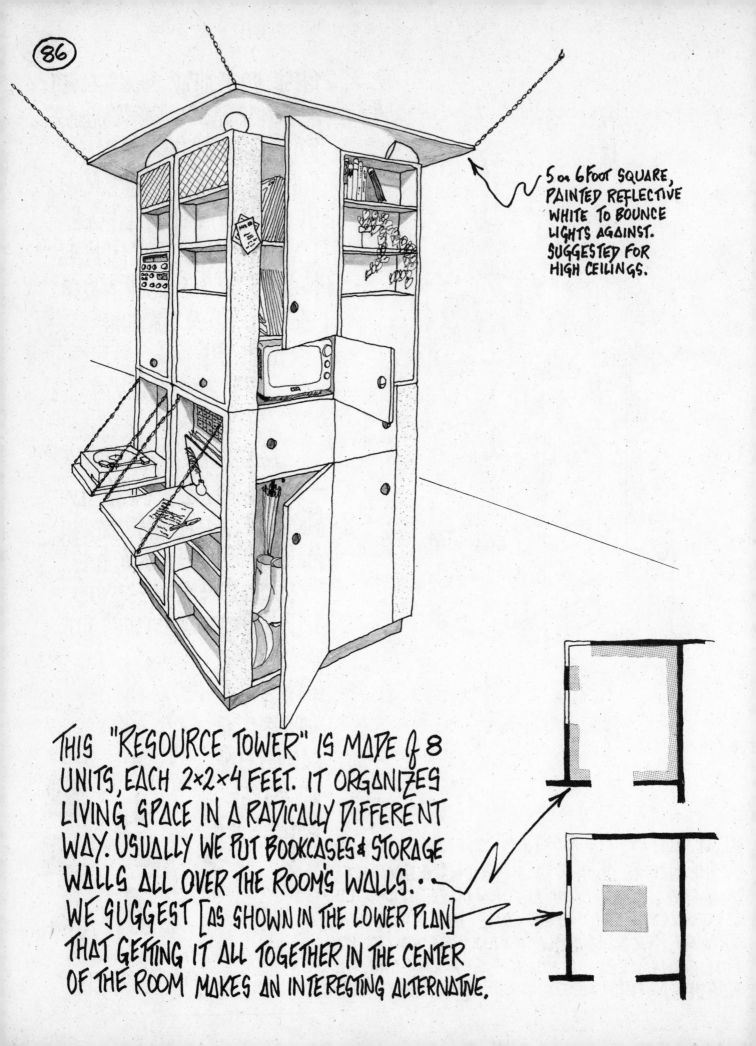

5 or 6 FOOT SQUARE, PAINTED REFLECTIVE WHITE TO BOUNCE LIGHTS AGAINST. SUGGESTED FOR HIGH CEILINGS.

THIS "RESOURCE TOWER" IS MADE of 8 UNITS, EACH 2×2×4 FEET. IT ORGANIZES LIVING SPACE IN A RADICALLY DIFFERENT WAY. USUALLY WE PUT BOOKCASES & STORAGE WALLS ALL OVER THE ROOM'S WALLS.·· WE SUGGEST [AS SHOWN IN THE LOWER PLAN] THAT GETTING IT ALL TOGETHER IN THE CENTER OF THE ROOM MAKES AN INTERESTING ALTERNATIVE.

# SHELF & CABINET UNIT → MAKE 8 FOR "TOWER":

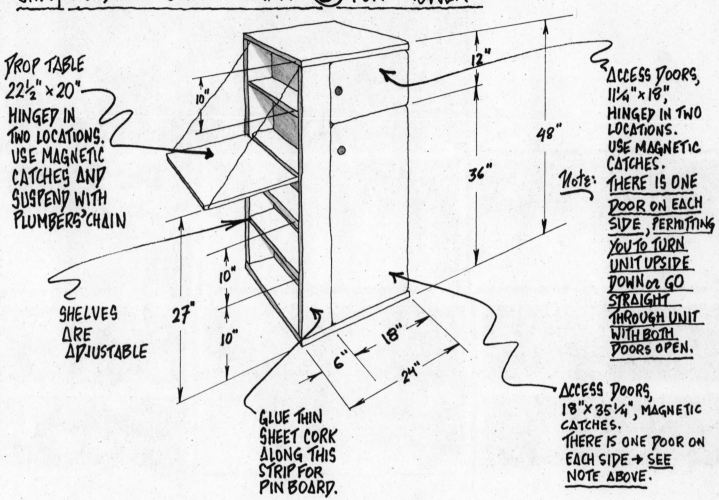

DROP TABLE 22½" × 20" HINGED IN TWO LOCATIONS. USE MAGNETIC CATCHES AND SUSPEND WITH PLUMBERS' CHAIN

SHELVES ARE ADJUSTABLE

10"

27"

10"

10"

6" · 18" · 24"

12"

48"

36"

ACCESS DOORS, 11¼" × 18", HINGED IN TWO LOCATIONS. USE MAGNETIC CATCHES. Note: THERE IS ONE DOOR ON EACH SIDE, PERMITTING YOU TO TURN UNIT UPSIDE DOWN or GO STRAIGHT THROUGH UNIT WITH BOTH DOORS OPEN.

GLUE THIN SHEET CORK ALONG THIS STRIP FOR PIN BOARD.

ACCESS DOORS, 18" × 35¼", MAGNETIC CATCHES. THERE IS ONE DOOR ON EACH SIDE → SEE NOTE ABOVE.

## BASE UNIT: MOUNT THE FOUR BOTTOM UNITS ON THIS WITH A 3" OVERHANG ALL AROUND. THEN MOUNT FOUR TOP UNITS TO COMPLETE TOWER.

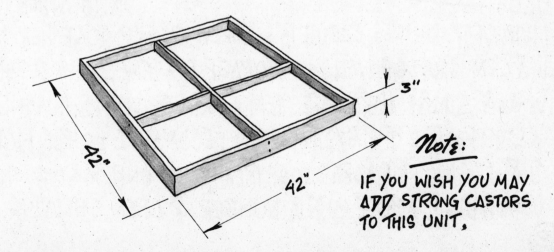

42"

42"

3"

Note:

IF YOU WISH YOU MAY ADD STRONG CASTORS TO THIS UNIT.

# ABOUT CONNECTORS:

LITERALLY HUNDREDS OF CONNECTOR-SYSTEMS EXIST WITH WHICH IT IS POSSIBLE TO STICK SHELVES, CABINETS or SHELVING UNITS TOGETHER IN ORDER TO FORM STORAGE WALLS or STORAGE SYSTEMS. ALL OF THESE DEPEND ON SOME SIMPLE HARDWARE ITEM & PRE~DRILLED SHELVING  — THE BUILDING OF THE SYSTEM THEN BECOMES A SIMPLE MATTER OF PLUGGING THE PARTS TOGETHER [AND UNPLUGGING THEM FOR MOVING]. ABOVE ARE A NUMBER OF OPEN SHELVING MODULES

**T U L +**

**✳**

OTHER
POSSIBLE
VARIATIONS
OF THIS
CONNECTOR

AND A DOUBLE~DOOR CABINET. THESE PARTS ARE MADE of PARTICLE~BOARD, COVERED WITH PAPER-THIN VENEER & PRE~DRILLED.

THE TWO PICTURES ABOVE SHOW THE STEEL CONNEC~TORS IN PLACE, AS WELL AS THE HOLES. THIS PARTICULAR SYSTEM WAS DESIGNED BY PETER OPSVIK, N.I.L. for A/S STRANDA of NORWAY. ◄

WE HAVE ALSO SHOWN SMALL SKETCHES of OTHER CONNECTORS IN THE SYSTEM, ABOVE LEFT.

→ HERE IS ANOTHER GOOD SYSTEM-ELEMENT:

← TO USE THIS CONNECTOR, A HOLE IS DRILLED INTO THE WOOD AND THE CONNECTOR IS SCREWED IN. THE CONNECTOR COMES IN SEVERAL SIZES & ACCEPTS MACHINE SCREWS ! GREAT FOR BLIND HOLES!

→ MADE BY: ROSAN INC.
2901 W. COAST HIGHWAY
NEWPORT BEACH, CALIFORNIA

↰ THIS IS ONE of THE MOST COMMON CONNECTORS TO BE FOUND. HAMMER IT INTO A DRILLED HOLE & INSERT A MACHINE SCREW FROM THE OTHER SIDE. IT IS CALLED A "T" NUT

THIS "T" BAR IS A METAL ROD WITH A TAPPED HOLE → A SIMPLE AND EFFECTIVE LOCKING DEVICE.

AVAILABLE AT MOST HARDWARE STORES.

# SPRING~LOADED POLE SYSTEMS:

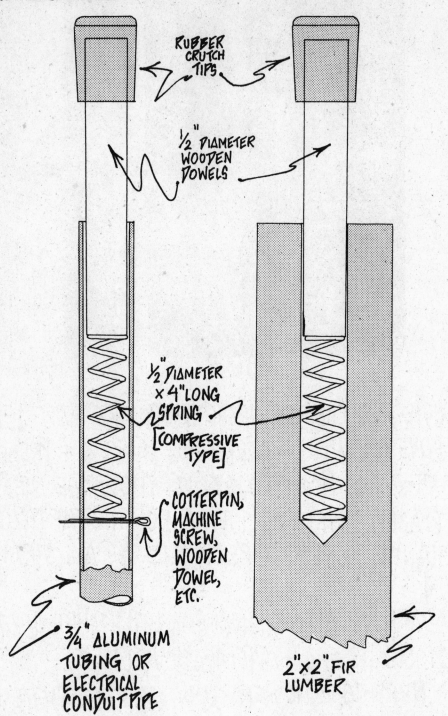

RUBBER CRUTCH TIPS

½" DIAMETER WOODEN DOWELS

½" DIAMETER × 4" LONG SPRING [COMPRESSIVE TYPE]

COTTER PIN, MACHINE SCREW, WOODEN DOWEL, ETC.

¾" ALUMINUM TUBING OR ELECTRICAL CONDUIT PIPE

2"×2" FIR LUMBER

THE MOST COMMON WAY OF HANGING SHELVING BETWEEN 2 ALUMINUM POLES IS TO DRILL CLEARANCE HOLES THROUGH CENTER, 1" IN FROM EACH NARROW SIDE & PUT THE SHELVES OVER THE POLES ["THREADING THEM ON"] BEFORE ERECTING THE POLES.

SHELVES CAN BE ATTACHED TO 2"×2"S WITH SHELF CLIPS [PAGE 75], BOB MOORE'S FRICTION FASTENERS [PAGE 94], OR ANY OTHER FASTENING METHOD YOU LIKE.
THE POLES CAN BE DRILLED THROUGH AT SHELF INTERVALS, WOODEN or METAL DOWELS CAN BE USED AS SHELF-RESTS.

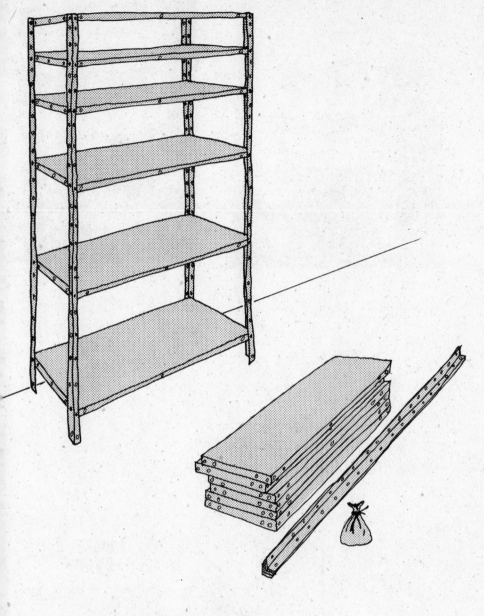

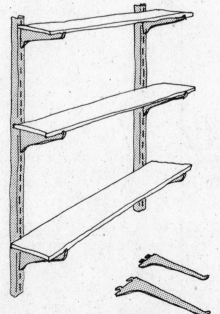

THERE ARE A NUMBER OF INDUSTRIAL SHELVING UNITS ON THE MARKET, USUALLY MADE OF STEEL WITH A DARK-GREEN OR GRAY BAKED ENAMEL FINISH.

THE ONE WE HAVE SHOWN IS THE SIMPLEST, UPRIGHTS & SHELVES COME IN MANY DIFFERENT SIZES. YOU CAN OFTEN FIND THESE UNITS SECOND-HAND, IF YOU LOOK IN STORES SELLING WAREHOUSE & SHOP FIXTURES.

BRACKETS & STANDARDS SUCH AS THESE ALSO ARE AVAILABLE IN MANY SIZES & COLOURS. → SEARS, HARDWARE STORES, LUMBER-YARDS & STORE FIXTURE SHOPS ARE THE SOURCES.

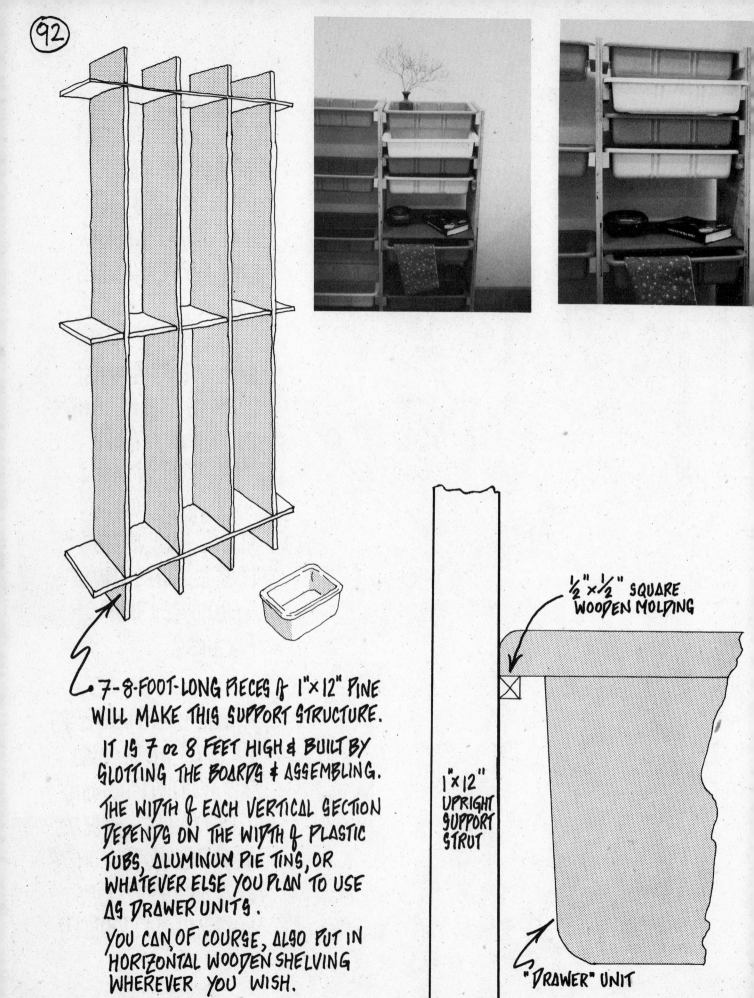

7-8-FOOT-LONG PIECES of 1"×12" PINE
WILL MAKE THIS SUPPORT STRUCTURE.

IT IS 7 or 8 FEET HIGH & BUILT BY
SLOTTING THE BOARDS & ASSEMBLING.

THE WIDTH of EACH VERTICAL SECTION
DEPENDS ON THE WIDTH of PLASTIC
TUBS, ALUMINUM PIE TINS, OR
WHATEVER ELSE YOU PLAN TO USE
AS DRAWER UNITS.

YOU CAN, OF COURSE, ALSO PUT IN
HORIZONTAL WOODEN SHELVING
WHEREVER YOU WISH.

½"×½" SQUARE
WOODEN MOLDING

1"×12"
UPRIGHT
SUPPORT
STRUT

"DRAWER" UNIT

THIS FREE~STANDING UNIT WAS BUILT BY JIM WHEN HE FIRST MOVED TO LOS ANGELES FROM SWEDEN.

IT IS ABSURDLY SIMPLE & PRACTICAL: THE END UNITS ARE TWO FLAT, WOODEN PEPSI~ COLA CASES, STANDING ON THE NARROW EDGES & FACING INWARD. THE SHELVING IS PRESSBOARD, WITH ALL BUT THE TOP AND THE CENTER SHELF, TONGUED TO FIT THE PEPSI CASES. PLASTIC TUBS HOLD LINENS, TOYS, ETC. WHEN MOVING, JIM CAN RECYCLE THE CASES & SHELVES & USE THE PLASTIC TUBS TO MOVE.

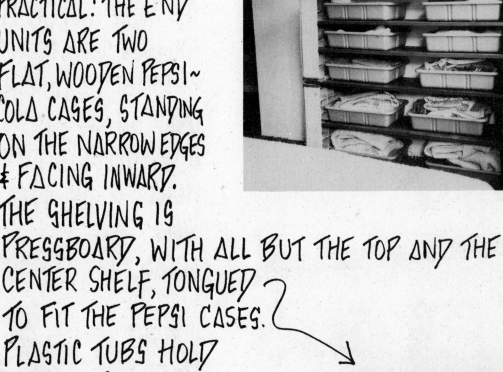

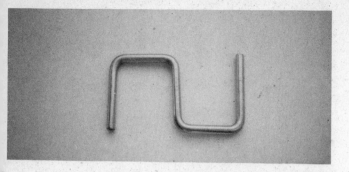

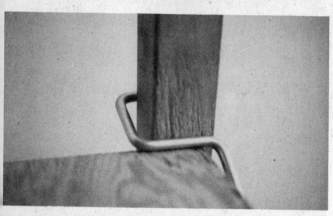

BOB MOORE, ONE of OUR GRADUATE STUDENTS, WHO CAME from ENGINEERING AT BERKELEY, DEVELOPED THIS FRICTION LOCKING CLAMP. IT IS A BEAUTIFULLY SIMPLE & ELEGANT WAY TO SUPPORT BOOKSHELVING.

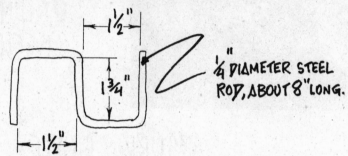

¼" DIAMETER STEEL ROD, ABOUT 8" LONG.

THE MORE WEIGHT IS PUT ON THE SHELVES, THE STRONGER THE SUPPORT BECOMES. IN OUR PICTURES IT IS USED ON 1½" x 1½" WOODEN UPRIGHTS AND SUPPORTS ¾" SHELVING. HOWEVER, THE SYSTEM WILL WORK EQUALLY WELL ON UPRIGHT POLES.

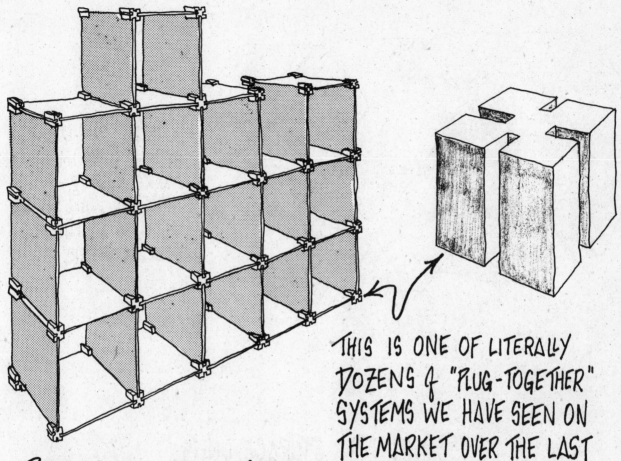

THIS IS ONE OF LITERALLY
DOZENS of "PLUG-TOGETHER"
SYSTEMS WE HAVE SEEN ON
THE MARKET OVER THE LAST
DOZEN YEARS or SO. IN THIS PARTICULAR SYSTEM BY DIETER
SCHEMPP of GERMANY THE PLANES ARE PAINTED PLYWOOD
& THE CONNECTORS A'RE BLACK PLASTIC.
                    OF PARTICULAR NOTE
ARE SIMILAR SYSTEMS, WITH PANELS IN GLASS AND/or CLEAR
PLASTIC, AVAILABLE FROM: ▶ THE DOOR STORE & BON MARCHÉ,
BOTH IN NEW YORK CITY.

THESE PLASTIC PIPE FITTINGS, WITH
A DIAMETER of LESS THAN 1½", ARE AVAILABLE
AT MOST HARDWARE STORES. WITH PLASTIC
PIPES, OR ALUMINUM or STEEL TUBING, THEY
CAN BUILD UP INTO SHELVING STRUTS,
JUNGLE-GYMS, OR INTO OUR CUBES [pp.79-81]

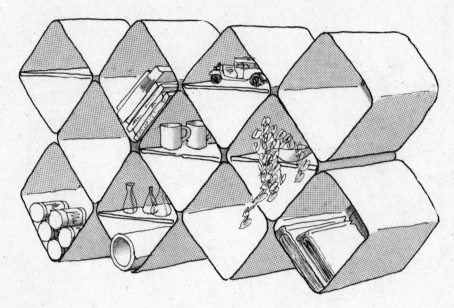

SQUARE TIN OIL
STORAGE DRUMS
MAKE A GOOD
HANGING WALL SHELF,
STANDING UNIT or
SPACE DIVIDER

## TIN-CAN STORAGE UNITS

THIS UNIT WILL STORE ROLLED-UP
POSTERS, DRAWINGS, ETC., OR
LARGER CANS WILL ACCOMMODATE
WINE BOTTLES.

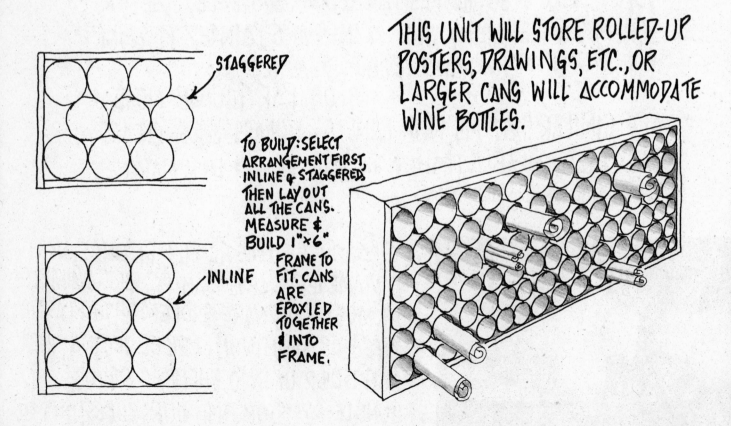

STAGGERED

INLINE

TO BUILD: SELECT
ARRANGEMENT FIRST,
INLINE & STAGGERED,
THEN LAY OUT
ALL THE CANS.
MEASURE &
BUILD 1"×6"
FRAME TO
FIT. CANS
ARE
EPOXIED
TOGETHER
& INTO
FRAME.

THIS SHOWS YOU HOW TO TURN THE DEAD END OF
A ROOM INTO A CLOTHES & UTILITY CLOSET. FIRST
RIP STANDARD 4×8-FOOT SHEETS OF PLYWOOD (¾")
OR FIBRE-CHIP-BOARD, INTO SECTIONS 2×8 FEET.
THESE FORM THE UPRIGHTS. A 1½" OR 2" STEEL PIPE,
SECURED WITH PIPE FLANGES, WILL SERVE AS A CLOTHES
ROD. YOU CAN NOW ALSO INSTALL SHELVES, AND
USE PLASTIC TRAYS OR BOXES AS DRAWERS,
[SEE PAGES 92-93].

YOU CAN ALSO HIDE ALL THIS FROM
VIEW, AND AT THE SAME TIME PROTECT
YOUR THINGS FROM DUST BY RUNNING
A FLOOR-TO-CEILING CURTAIN FROM A
CEILING TRACK IN FRONT OF THE UNIT.

PLAN VIEW OF ROOM, SHOWING CLOSET NICHE.

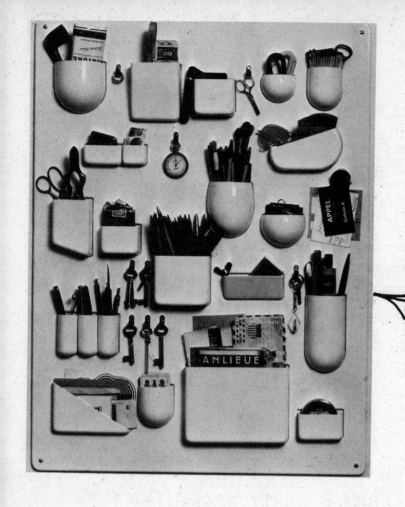

THIS ATTRACTIVE "WALL POCKET"
COMES IN A HARD PLASTIC IN
BRIGHT RED, WHITE, YELLOW,
OR BLACK. IT IS 34 × 26½
INCHES. HOWEVER IT ALSO
CARRIES A PRICE~TAG of
NEARLY $50.~ !

→ WE SUGGEST THAT YOU CAN
SEW SIMILAR PANELS, OUT of
CANVAS or LINEN IN NATURAL
or BRIGHT COLOURS. MAKE
THEM 48" WIDE & PROVIDE
BRASS GROMMETS.
THEN YOU CAN "BUTTON"
THEM TO WALLS, "TOWERS," or
OUR CUBES [PAGES 79-81, 86, 87],
OR USE THEM AS SPACE-DIVIDERS.

# SLEEPING+ :

BEDS ARE NOT JUST TO SLEEP IN. WE GO TO BED TO REST, TO MAKE LOVE, SOMETIMES BECAUSE WE ARE ILL.

TRADITIONAL JAPAN HAD ANSWERS FOR THIS, AS FOR SO MANY OTHER PROBLEMS IN DOMESTIC ARCHITEC~ TURE: A FLOOR COVERED WITH *TATAMI* WAS BOTH FLOOR AND BED. TO THIS MIGHT BE ADDED A SORT OF SOFT SLEEPING~BAG FOR THE NIGHT: *FUTON*. BUT SUCH CONCEPTS CANNOT BE RIPPED OUT OF ONE CULTURE AND WORK IN ANOTHER — THEY LOSE TOO MUCH IN TRANSLATION.*

UNTIL A FEW HUNDRED YEARS AGO, CIVILIZED EUROPEANS SLEPT SITTING UP. MANY MEMBERS OF THE AMERICAN YOUTH SUBCULTURE CARRY SLEEPING BAGS AS ROUTINELY AS THEIR ELDERS CARRY AN AMERICAN EXPRESS CARD.

BUT THESE ARE ALL SOLUTIONS TOO SPECIALIZED, TOO WELL KNOWN, OR TOO IMPRACTICAL TO BE SHOWN HERE.

VIC & JIM DID A GREAT DEAL OF RESEARCH ON SLEEPING ARRANGEMENTS THAT ARE COMPATIBLE WITH

*FOR AN EXPLANATION OF WHY SUCH TRANSLATIONS DON'T WORK, SEE VIC'S "DESIGN FOR THE REAL WORLD", pp. 13-14.

A MORE NOMADIC LIFE~STYLE. BUT THE FOLLOWING PAGES DON'T REFLECT THIS RESEARCH. AFTER LOOKING THROUGH HUNDREDS OF BOOKS, MAGAZINES & MANU~FACTURERS' CATALOGS, WE FOUND THAT BEDS ARE JUST A QUESTION OF STYLING OR APPEARANCE DESIGN, IN OTHER WORDS: SURFACE COSMETICS.

THE PUBLIC IS GIVEN A "CHOICE" BETWEEN INNER~SPRING & VARIOUS COIL MATTRESSES OR FOAM. THERE IS THE FURTHER CHOICE OF SIZE AND, IF LIVING IN HOLLYWOOD: ROUND BEDS.

BASICALLY THE ONLY REAL DIFFERENCES HAVE TO DO WITH LOOKS. HENCE "EARLY AMERICAN", "FRENCH PROVINCIAL", "BAUHAUS~MODERNE" AND PROBABLY EVEN "JAVANESE COLONIAL" HEADBOARDS, FRAMES & NIGHT TABLES ABOUND. VIC, WHO HAS A PERVERSE INTEREST IN SUCH THINGS, RECENTLY FOUND A BED, THE FRAME OF WHICH WAS CONSTRUCTED OF PINK TRANSPARENT PLASTIC FAKE BAMBOO, TORTURED INTO THE OVERBLOWN CURVES OF BAVARIAN BAROQUE. THIS WRETCHED HORROR WAS COVERED WITH A BEDSPREAD WHICH WAS AN IMITATION NAVAJO RUG, CONFECTED OF FAKE PLASTIC FUR IN ORANGE, LIGHT BLUE & A BROWN OF THE EXACT COLOURING OF MILK CHOCOLATE!

ENOUGH. BEGINNING ON THE NEXT PAGE WE HAVE A FEW [A VERY FEW] IDEAS FOR BEDS THAT MAKE SENSE. IF YOU ARE CAUGHT UP WITH HEADBOARDS, WE SUGGEST ANY GOOD TEXT ON INFERIOR DESECRATION.

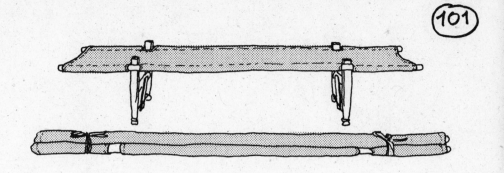

This remarkably ingenious roll-up bed is made of beechwood and linen-canvas. It uses rope and a wooden stop, to achieve tension through the principle of the bucksaw [see detail, left below]. It was designed by Ole Gjerløv-Knudsen of Denmark, who also designed the chair using the bucksaw principle, on page 16.
▶ Available from: "Interna," Copenhagen, Denmark.

Harlanne & Vic have slept on beds like this in Sweden for four months → they are unbelievably comfortable.

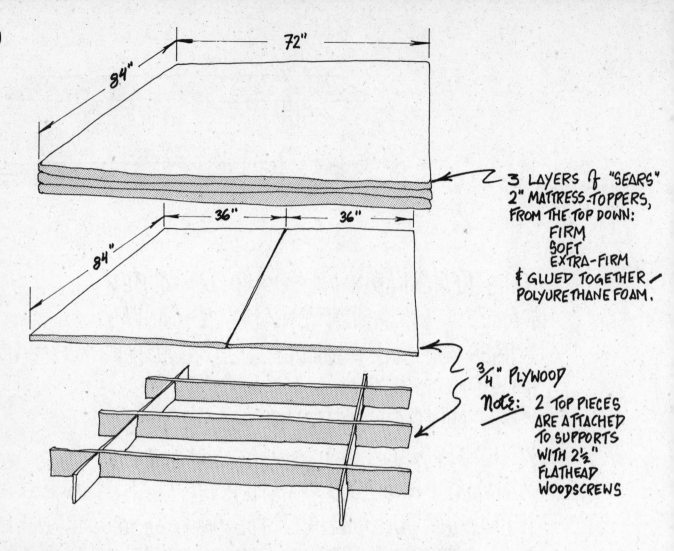

72"

84"

3 LAYERS of "SEARS"
2" MATTRESS-TOPPERS,
FROM THE TOP DOWN:
    FIRM
    SOFT
    EXTRA-FIRM
& GLUED TOGETHER /
POLYURETHANE FOAM.

36"    36"

84"

$\frac{3}{4}$" PLYWOOD

Note: 2 TOP PIECES
ARE ATTACHED
TO SUPPORTS
WITH 2$\frac{1}{2}$"
FLATHEAD
WOODSCREWS

THE COMPLETED
BED, COVERED
WITH marimekko
COTTON PRINT.

THE BED IS
EXTRA LARGE,
SO-CALLED
"CALIFORNIA
KING-SIZE",
72" x 84."

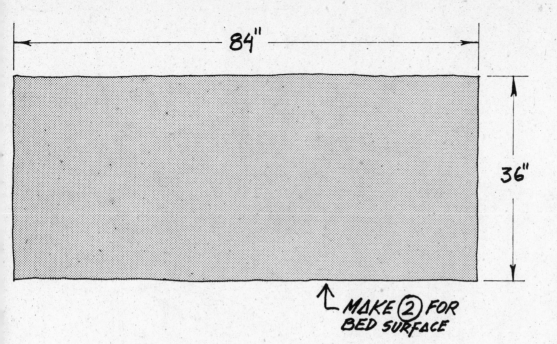

84"

36"

↳ MAKE ②　FOR
BED SURFACE

# FOAM BED

POLYURETHANE FOAM, RESTING DIRECTLY ON ¾" PLYWOOD, PROVIDES RESTFUL AND HEALTHY SLEEP~SUPPORT. VIC'S BED [SEE PHOTO] IS EXTRA LARGE, THE FOAM MATTRESS, WHICH WOULD GIVE AN EVEN DENSITY ⨍ 5 INCHES HAS BEEN DISCARDED IN FAVOUR ⨍ THREE "MATTRESS-TOPPERS", EACH 2 INCHES THICK AND ⨍ DIFFERING

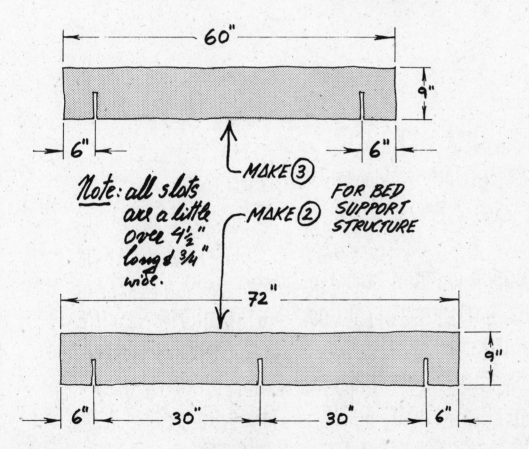

60"

9"

6"　　　6"

↳ MAKE ③

Note: all slots are a little over 4½" long & ¾" wide.

MAKE ②　FOR BED SUPPORT STRUCTURE

72"

9"

6"　　30"　　30"　　6"

NOTE:
CHANGE ALL SIZES PROPORTIONATELY TO FIT YOUR MATTRESS NEEDS.

DENSITIES.
　THE TWO SURFACE TOPPERS CAN BE MADE ⨍ ¾" PLYWOOD OR CHIP-BOARD. THE LEG~SUBSTRUCTURE CAN ALSO BE MADE ⨍ ¾" PLY, or else OF SHELVING LUMBER. SUB~ STRUCTURE IS SET IN 6 INCHES FROM ALL SIDES.

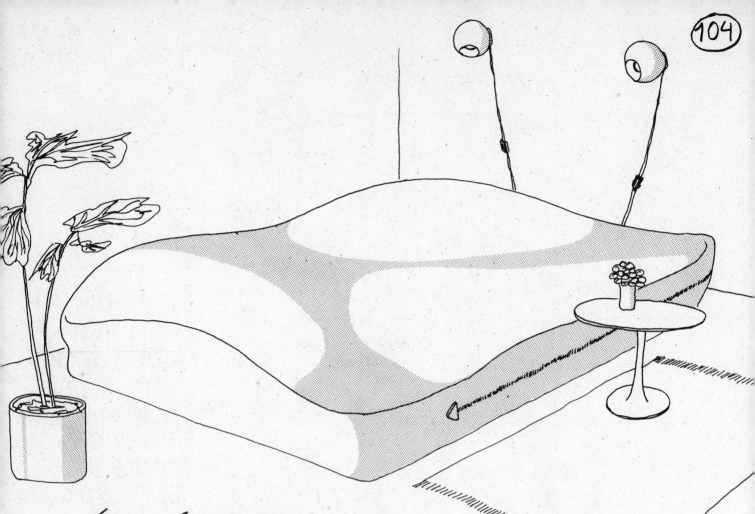

THIS IS THE BEANBAG CHAIR,
ENLARGED TO BECOME A GIGANTIC CUSHION,
MEASURING 54" x 78" AND ABOUT 7" THICK. YOU WILL
NEED ABOUT 7 TO 8 YARDS of 60"-WIDE CLOSE~WOVEN FABRIC,
THE SAME LENGTH & WIDTH of MUSLIN [FOR THE INNER BAG] AND
TWO HEAVY 72" ZIPPERS. FOLLOW OUR INSTRUCTIONS FOR THE
BEAN~BAG CHAIR ON PAGE 29. THE BED IS STUFFED WITH
ABOUT 25-30 POUNDS of SHREDDED FOAM, WHICH IS INEX-
PENSIVELY AVAILABLE AT WAR~SURPLUS STORES. BE SURE TO TEAR
THE PLASTIC BAG of SHREDDED FOAM ALONG ONE SIDE AND PLACE
INSIDE MUSLIN BAG BEFORE EMPTYING IT. THIS MATTRESS RESTS
ON THE FLOOR, BUT YOU MAY ALSO BUILD A BASE FOR IT.
→ ALTERNATIVE: STUFF IT WITH PLASTIC PELLETS LIKE THE CHAIR.

Note: THE TWO SPOTLAMPS ABOVE THE BED ARE ON PAGE 119.

IN OUR SOCIETY WE THINK OF HAMMOCKS
AS EXCLUSIVELY OCCUPIED BY MIDDLE-AGED,
BALD MEN ~ FITTING TARGETS FOR
WATERHOSES FIENDISHLY EMPLOYED BY LITTLE BOYS.
SAILORS AND PEOPLE IN THE WEST INDIES KNOW THEM
TO BE SUPERBLY NOMADIC BEDS.

# WATER-BEDS:

WATER-BEDS REALLY ARE AN EXCELLENT, NEW WAY of RESTING, SLEEPING, ETC.

WE HAVE JUST A FEW SUGGESTIONS:

1. <u>BEFORE YOU BUY</u> A WATER~BED, MAKE SURE THAT YOUR FLOOR CAN SUPPORT THE 1600 LBS. IT WILL WEIGH WHEN FILLED.

2. <u>BEFORE YOU FILL IT</u>, DECIDE EXACTLY WHERE IT WILL STAND. IT'S HARD TO MOVE 1600 POUNDS!

3. DON'T BUY A PLASTIC WATER~BAG THAT <u>CLAIMS</u> TO BE A WATER-BED. THESE RIP~OFFS SELL FOR ANYWHERE FROM $8⁹⁵ TO $49⁹⁵ AND AREN'T WORTH IT.

THIS IS WHY WE HAVE TAKEN THE UNUSUAL STEP of REPRODUCING THIS FULL-PAGE ADVERTISEMENT. <u>READ IT CAREFULLY</u> & CON~ SIDER BUYING THEIR PRODUCT.

4. IF YOU HAVE THE SKILL, BUILD YOUR OWN, BUT MAKE SURE THAT IT HAS ALL THE FEATURES OF THE ONE FROM *"INNERSPACE,"* OR MORE.

# The truth about waterbeds.

## by Irving London, M.D.

**SAVE THIS PAGE**–because 4 in 5 of us may eventually sleep on a patented, heated waterbed. Let this be your guide to the most comfortable, healthful, natural, sleeping surface ever created.

With the invention of the waterbed by Innerspace Environments has come a myriad of myths and rumors. Here, I intend to present the truth concerning this remarkable advancement in sleep technology.

I've been sleeping on a proper waterbed for over 2 years, and it has dramatically changed my life for the better. If that seems to be overstating things, I promise you it is true.

I purchased an Innerspace Bed because I hoped its even support and gentle heat could relax and soothe my bad back. The results were so positive, I decided to devote the majority of my time to the science of sleep, and the contribution the waterbed has made to this science. I felt I could be of more service to more people this way rather than by devoting all my time to the practice of medicine.

### WHO SHOULD BUY A WATERBED?

Actually, everyone who sleeps should at least consider a waterbed.

You should seriously look in to buying the Innerspace Bed if you are a person with a back problem or aching muscles. People with these problems, plus people with insomnia, nervous tension or anxiety have often found the Innerspace Bed extremely beneficial. Sleep comes easier. Many people gain deep, restful sleep without medication. And certainly, people who sleep better, look better.

You should also consider a waterbed for the superb sleep and natural comfort it affords. A prime quality, heated waterbed can give you the exquisite sensation of semi-weightlessness.

A recent independent consumer research study revealed that 93% of owners of the Innerspace Bed intend to sleep on a heated waterbed every night for the rest of their lives.

### DON'T CONFUSE A WATERBED WITH A WATERBAG.

Be sure you get an authentic heated waterbed, not a waterbag.

To be certain you get a proper waterbed, look for a patented model. The patent makes all the difference. It assures you of a bed that has been bio-engineered, using a unique liquid support system for comfort and therapeutic merit.

The Innerspace Bed (U.S. Patent Number 3,585,356) is a heavy-duty vinyl mattress, filled with water kept at the temperature you desire by an

### THE WATERBAG

① Vinyl mattress.

### THE WATERBED:

① Heavy duty vinyl mattress.
② Watertight casing.
③ Heating unit.
④ Frame.
⑤ Thermostat.
⑥ Raised base.

adjustable, automatic heating unit.

The mattress rests in a watertight casing; the entire unit is contained in a specially-crafted frame atop a raised base.

A waterbag is a vinyl bag of water.

### COMPARE A PATENTED WATERBED WITH ANY CONVENTIONAL BED MADE.

A waterbed supports and cushions your entire body evenly. A conventional bed

does not. A waterbed supports the small of your back, where you need support most. A conventional bed does not.

Most importantly, a conventional bed creates pressure points which cut off blood flow and cause tossing and turning. On a waterbed, there can be no pressure points.

Many people who sleep on the Innerspace Bed report that they fall asleep and awaken in the same position.

**The conventional bed : partial support**

**The Innerspace Bed : total support**

Compare this with a conventional bed where the average person changes position 50 to 80 times a night! Numerous owners of the Innerspace Bed claim they actually need fewer hours of sleep.

A heated waterbed warms you with the same heat principle employed by

hospitals with hydrotherapy. Such penetrating, relaxing warmth is impossible with a conventional bed, even with electric blankets. Even more, a waterbed can keep you cool during hot weather; simply adjust the thermostat to a cooler temperature.

### SAFETY CONSIDERATIONS.

Innerspace Environments manufactures the only waterbeds listed by Underwriters' Laboratories, an independent, not-for-profit organization testing for public safety. UL listed the Innerspace Bed as "safeguarded to an acceptable degree . . . with respect to all reasonably foreseeable hazards to life and property."

The Innerspace Bed has also been approved by The Electrical Testing Laboratory of the City of Los Angeles, and the Canadian Standards Association, a branch of the Canadian government.

No other waterbed has passed all these rigorous examinations.

The patented construction of the Innerspace Bed makes it acceptable to landlords. Placed against a wall, as virtually all beds are, the Innerspace Bed is safely within minimum FHA weight limits.

### A NOTE TO NEWLYWEDS.

Because you will spend about ⅓ of your life in bed, your bed will be one of the most important purchases you make. So be careful you do not buy obsolescence. Many experts estimate that within 5 to 10 years, the majority of Americans will be sleeping on a heated waterbed.

### SOME FRANK ADVICE.

It is not possible to put into words the remarkable difference a waterbed makes. So I hope you will stretch out on a waterbed, and feel the astounding comfort for yourself.

Innerspace Environments offers a choice of waterbeds to fit any decor. Buying a waterbed is made as easy as possible. A selection of financing plans is offered. Master Charge and Bank-Americard are accepted. Prices start at under $200 for a complete unit.

Discover why the Innerspace Bed has become the most accepted, most popular waterbed in the world. Come in to an Innerspace showroom and experience the most sleepable bed ever invented.

It can change your life, too.

"... a giant leap forward in bed design."
**BETTER HOMES AND GARDENS**

"... patients expressed a preference for the waterbed because they were more comfortable on it."
**AMERICAN JOURNAL OF PHYSICAL MEDICINE**

"One of the most revolutionary ideas in sleep comfort ... emulates nature."
**LOS ANGELES TIMES**

"... we're convinced they will eventually rival, if not replace, innerspring mattresses, the same way that TV zapped radio."
**MONEYSWORTH, THE CONSUMER NEWSLETTER**

"Buyers with bad backs report noticeable relief ... the waterbed seems well on its way towards becoming a permanent fixture."
**TIME**

"... comfort is unsurpassed."
**WALL STREET JOURNAL**

**West Hollywood:** 951 North La Cienega Blvd., Los Angeles Phone: 659-4414

**Studio City:** 12301 Ventura Blvd., Studio City Phone: 980-9150

**Wilshire Center:** 3150-52 Wilshire Blvd., Los Angeles Phone: 487-4204

**Marina Del Rey:** 409 Washington St., Venice Phone: 821-8053

**Del Amo:** 180 Del Amo Fashion Square Torrance • Phone: 370-5557

All stores now open 7 days a week.

R-1

© **Innerspace**

THE CORPORATION THAT INVENTED, PATENTED, PERFECTED THE WATERBED.

THE NORTH FACE

ALPINE EQUIPMENT SPECIALIST

FINALLY A WORD ABOUT SLEEPING BAGS: OF THE MANY VIC HAS TESTED, THIS ONE BY "NORTH FACE" IS BY FAR THE BEST.
IT IS CALLED THE "SUPERLIGHT" AND IS STUFFED WITH PRIME NORTHERN EUROPEAN GOOSE DOWN. IN IT YOU CAN LIVE WITH TEMPERATURES AS LOW AS 10°F., YET IT WEIGHS ONLY THREE POUNDS!

IT COMES IN TWO SIZES [REGULAR & LARGE], TWO BAGS CAN BE ZIPPED TOGETHER TO FORM A DOUBLE. CONSIDERING THE BAG'S SUPERB WORKMANSHIP & QUALITY, IT IS QUITE REASONABLE AT $81.— ▶ ORDER FROM THE NORTH FACE, P.O. BOX 2399, STATION A BERKELEY, CALIF. 94702. ▶ THEY ALSO SELL OTHER BAGS, BACKPACKS, ETC.

# LIGHT:

• DIRECT LIGHTING MEANS A BEAM OF LIGHT ON YOUR WORK AREA, THE BOOK YOU ARE READING, ETC.

• INDIRECT LIGHTING MEANS THAT THE ACTUAL LIGHT-SOURCE IS USUALLY CONCEALED AND THE BEAM OF LIGHT IS DIRECTED AT A BRIGHT REFLECTIVE SURFACE [OFTEN UPWARDS TOWARD THE CEILING] AND IS THEN REFLECTED BACK TOWARD YOU.

• DIFFUSED LIGHT MEANS THAT THE BULB OR BULBS ARE BEHIND A SEMI-TRANSPARENT MATERIAL THROUGH WHICH THE BULB IS NOT VISIBLE, BUT LIGHT IS PERMITTED TO FILTER THROUGH (FOR EXAMPLE: MILK GLASS, PARCHMENT PAPER, THIN CLOUDY SHEET PLASTIC, ETC.).

• "MOOD" LIGHTING COVERS A MULTITUDE OF SINS, FROM A SMALL WHITE BEDROOM GLOBE THAT IS GOVERNED BY A VARIABLE RHEOSTAT TO A 15"-HIGH FOUR-MASTED SCHOONER, HAND-CHEWED OUT OF ROSEWOOD, WITH CHROMIUM SAILS, BLINKING "CANDLE-FLICKER" RUNNING LIGHTS, AN ILLUMINATED CLOCK IN THE STERN, AND RESTING ON A CIRCULAR BLUE-TINTED MIRROR.

• MOST DOMESTIC LIGHTING COMBINES ALL FOUR OF THESE.

• ADDED TO WHICH MUST BE: SOME LAMPS ARE USED AS SCULPTURE ONLY. JUST DRIVE THROUGH ANY SUBDIVISION & YOU CAN SEE: A TABLE IN FRONT OF EVERY PICTURE WINDOW & IN THE EXACT CENTER OF THE TABLE AN ENORMOUSLY GROSS LAMP WITH A BILLOWING SHADE, RECALLING THE LACY FROU-FROU PETTICOATS OF A GAY NINETIES BAR IN ITCH, NEVADA.

WE HAVE ATTEMPTED TO SHOW AT LEAST ONE TYPE OF LIGHT FOR EACH OF THESE FOUR METHODS, AS WELL AS FOR THE "LAMP AS SCULPTURE" CONCEPT.

BECAUSE OF OUR OWN PERSONAL BIAS, WE FEEL THAT THE IDEAL MOOD LIGHT IS PROVIDED BY CANDLELIGHT. WE DO DRAW THE LINE HOWEVER AT "SCENTED" OR "PERFUMED" CANDLES WHICH EITHER GIVE OFF AN ODOUR OF STALE, MARIHUANA~SOAKED TENNIS SOCKS, OR ELSE FOLLOW THE "12-NIGHTS-ON-A-TROOPSHIP" PERFUME SYNDROME.

IN A WAY, DIRECT LIGHTING IS COMPARABLE TO WORK or DINING CHAIRS. BY THIS WE MEAN THAT GOOD, NOMADIC & INEXPENSIVE TYPES CAN BE BOUGHT NEARLY EVERYWHERE. NONETHELESS WE HAVE GIVEN ONE DOUBLE~LIGHT THAT YOU CAN BUILD OUT OF RE~CYCLED MILK BOTTLES.

OUR LIGHT~COLUMN & THE BASES FOR VARIOUS EXISTING BLEACH BOTTLES, MILK BOTTLES, GLOBES, ETC.; AS WELL AS THE STYROFOAM BUBBLE MADE OF OLD COFFEE CUPS; PROVIDE DIFFUSED LIGHT.

FOR INDIRECT LIGHTING, TURN ANY OF THE DIRECT FIXTURES TOWARD A WHITE WALL, OR ELSE BOUNCE THE LIGHT OFF THE CEILING. VIC HAS LIVED IN A HUGE HOUSE WITH ONLY 7 "LUXO" LAMPS FOR BOTH DIRECT & INDIRECT LIGHT.

BUT OUR "ELECTRIC SNAKE" WILL AGAIN SHOW YOU THAT THE ONLY LIMITS ARE YOUR OWN WILL TO TRY THE NEW.

# Bubble Lamp

MADE FROM OLD STYROFOAM CUPS. THIS IDEA HAS BY NOW BEEN USED BY YOUNG PEOPLE IN AUSTRIA, FINLAND, JAPAN, THE U.S.; IT IS VIRTUALLY A CLICHÉ.

STYROFOAM COFFEE CUPS COME IN MANY DIFFERENT SIZES → THE

SIZE CUP YOU USE WILL DETERMINE THE SIZE OF THE BUBBLE. THIS PARTICULAR ONE WAS MADE BY JIM, USING "STANDARD" CUPS [WHICH ARE FREE] AND IS ABOUT 42" IN DIAMETER. IT IS REALLY JUST A SHELL, SURROUNDING A HANGING BULB IN THE CENTER. SOME STYROFOAM CUPS ARE LITTLE LARGER THAN SHOT~GLASSES → RESULTING IN HOLLOW SPHERES OF ABOUT 26" DIAMETER. IF YOU ARE NEAR A SOURCE THAT USES GIANT MILK~SHAKE STYROFOAM CUPS, YOU CAN BUILD A GLOBE THAT IS NEARLY 6 FEET. BUT REMEMBER → IT WILL TAKE ABOUT 250 CUPS PER LAMP.
→ THE BEST WAY TO BUILD IT, IS TO USE WHITE ELMER'S GLUE, AND USE CLOTHES~PINS TO HOLD THE LAMP~PARTS TOGETHER, WHILE DRYING. SOME TIME AGO "ESQUIRE" SUGGESTED HEAT~SEALING THE CUPS TOGETHER, THIS DOESN'T WORK AS WELL. → TO GET A PERFECT SPHERE → START WITH ONE CUP & KEEP ADDING, DON'T BUILD 2 HALVES & TRY TO FIT THEM TOGETHER!

AT FIRST SIGHT YOU MAY NOT FIND THIS IDEA OF A LIGHT-COLUMN BY HARLANNE ALL THAT IMPRESSIVE.

BUT IT IS INCREDIBLY NOMADIC, INEXPENSIVE, EASY-TO-BUILD & VERY HANDSOME.

ALL OF OUR LIGHTING HERE CAN BE DIVIDED INTO THREE KINDS: DIRECT WORK-LIGHT, INDIRECT "MOOD" LIGHT & A COMBINATION OF THE TWO. THIS ONE GIVES INDIRECT LIGHT TO A LARGE [30 $26-FOOT] LIVING ROOM.

IT CONSISTS OF FIVE JAPANESE PAPER LANTERNS. FROM ALL OF THEM, EXCEPT THE TOP ONE, THE WIRE HANGING LOOP HAS BEEN REMOVED → ALL FIVE HAVE THEN BEEN TAPED TOGETHER & HUNG FROM AN EYE-HOOK IN THE CEILING. THE COLUMN IS 8 FEET TALL & COLLAPSES NEARLY FLAT [LIKE AN ACCORDION] FOR EASY MOVING. IT IS MUCH LESS DELICATE THAN IT LOOKS: WE HAVE MOVED IT FIVE TIMES, SOMETIMES ADDING AN EXTRA LANTERN FOR A HIGHER CEILING, SOMETIMES TAKING ONE OFF.

IT WEIGHS 1¾ LBS.

THE LIGHTING COMES FROM A STRING OF CHRISTMAS-TREE LIGHTS, WITH WHITE FROSTED BULBS INSTEAD OF COLOURED ONES.

FOR EXTRA "MOOD" LIGHTING, YOU CAN PLUG IT THROUGH A VARIABLE RHEOSTAT.

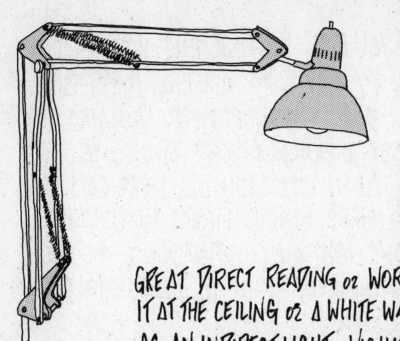

THIS IS THE OLD STANDBY, THE "LUXO" LAMP, ORIGINALLY DESIGNED IN SWEDEN. THE FACT THAT IT ADJUSTS AT NEARLY ANY ANGLE, SWIVELS FREELY THROUGH A COMPLETE 360° CIRCLE AND HAS 45-INCH ARM-REACH, MAKES IT A GREAT DIRECT READING or WORKING LIGHT. BY POINTING IT AT THE CEILING or A WHITE WALL, IT ALSO DOES DOUBLE DUTY AS AN INDIRECT LIGHT. VIC HAS BRACKETS FOR IT ALL OVER HIS HOUSE, WHICH MAKES IT POSSIBLE TO "UNPLUCK" A LAMP AND PLUG IT IN SOMEWHERE ELSE.

THE "LUXO" IS EXPENSIVE: NEARLY $30⁰⁰. HOWEVER, YOU CAN ORDER A "DO-IT-YOURSELF" KIT FOR $9⁰⁰

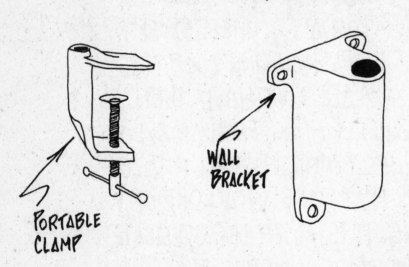

PORTABLE CLAMP

WALL BRACKET

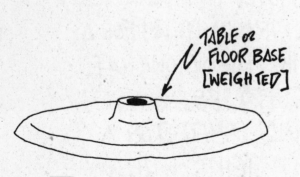

TABLE or FLOOR BASE [WEIGHTED]

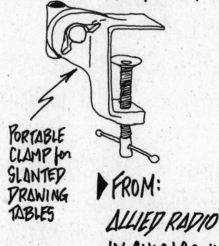

PORTABLE CLAMP for SLANTED DRAWING TABLES

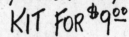

FROM: ALLIED RADIO IN CHICAGO, ILL.

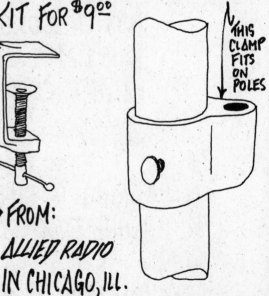

THIS CLAMP FITS ON POLES

"MOBILE"
DESIGNED
BY KAJA
AARIKKA
& AVAILABLE
FROM →
AARIKKA-
KORU,
FREDRIKINKATU
56D, HELSINKI
10, FINLAND

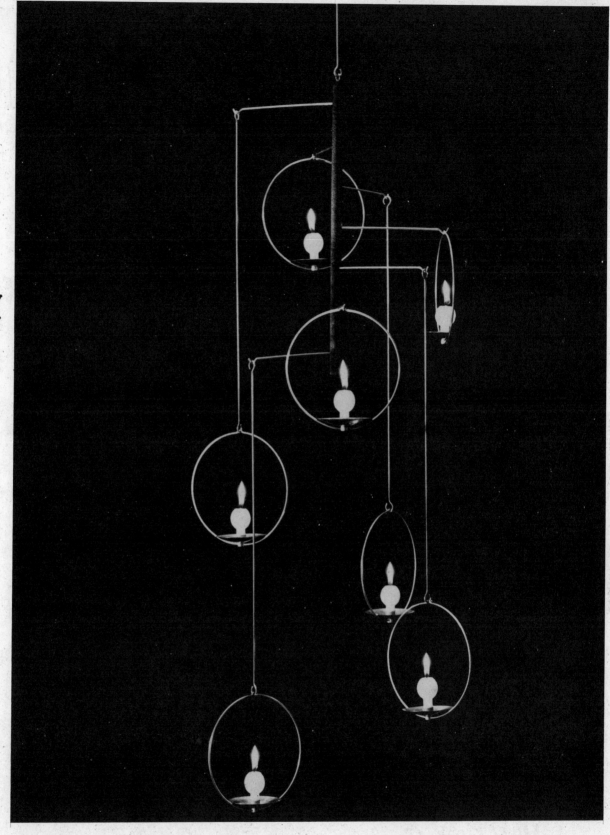

CANDLE-LIGHT IS LIKE FLOWERS, MUSIC AND BOOKS: A BASIC
NEED FOR MANY of US.
"MOBILE" MEANS MOVEMENT.
THERE IS LOTS & LOTS of WIRE IN THIS WORLD, PLUS YOUR
IMAGINATION.

PHOTO: COURTESY "DESIGN"

← THIS LAMP WAS DESIGNED BY THE LATE [& GREAT] JOE COLOMBO. FROM ITS EXCELLENT "MACHINE ~ AESTHETICS", A GOODLY NUMBER OF SALES HAVE ACCRUED TO ITS MANUFACTURER: O-LUCE OF MILANO, FROM WHOM THE UNIT IS AVAILABLE.

• MEANWHILE VIC HAS BEEN FASCINATED BY THE POLYETHYLENE BOTTLES WITH MOLDED HANDLES IN WHICH MILK IS SOLD IN SOUTHERN CALIFORNIA — [OTHER THINGS LIKE LAUNDRY DETERGENTS, PHOTO ~ CHEMICALS, ETC, ALSO COME IN THESE BOTTLES]. SO VIC DEVELOPED A LAMP, WHICH WE FEEL TO BE BETTER & ALSO AESTHETICALLY MORE PLEASING THAN THE O-LUCE ORIGINAL. THE TRANSLUCENT BOTTLES GIVE A MARVELOUS LIGHT QUALITY TO THESE RECYCLED MILK BOTTLES.

• JIM WORKED OUT THE ADJUSTABLE CONNECTORS & SUB~ STRUCTURE. SUGGESTION → DRILL ½" DIAMETER HOLES INTO TABLES & OTHER FURNITURE: YOU CERTAINLY WILL THEN BE ABLE TO PULL THE LAMP OUT OF ITS BASE & "PLUG" ITS MAIN POLE INTO OTHER LOCATIONS.

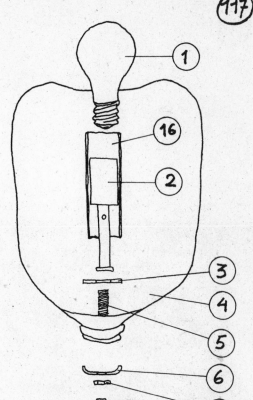

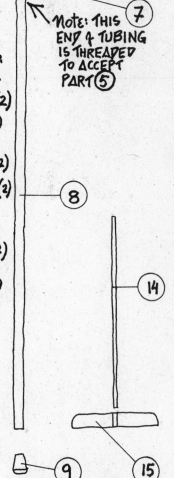

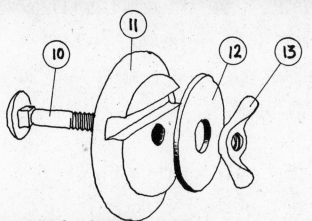

Note: THIS END OF TUBING IS THREADED TO ACCEPT PART (5)

## CONSTRUCTION OF STEM LOCKS:

DRILL A 1/4" CLEARANCE HOLE THROUGH KNOBS (11). SLOT EACH KNOB 3/8" WIDE AND 5/16" DEEP WITH A COPING SAW. SLOTS SHOULD BE JUST OFF CENTER HOLE. LOCK TWO KNOBS TOGETHER WITH (10), (12) & (13). — USE ABOUT 10 FEET OF LAMP CORD FOR EACH LAMP. MOUNT SEPARATE SWITCHES ON EACH CORD. WIRE BOTH CORDS TO THE SAME OUTLET PLUG.

WE HAVE PAINTED KNOBS (11) & BASE (15) FLAT BLACK.

→ PARTS SOURCE:

J.G. HOLZGANG, INC.
LOS ANGELES, CALIF. 90007

## ASSEMBLY INSTRUCTIONS:

1. BULB, MAXIM. 60 WATTS (2)
2. EXTENDED SOCKETS (2) HOLZGANG #S-9800
3. 1½" I.D.-3/16" O.D. WASHERS (2)
4. CUT POLYETHYLENE BOTTLES (2)
5. THREADED STUDS (2) HOLZGANG #S-1089
6. BRASS CAP WASHERS (2) HOLZGANG #S-1542
7. NUT/LOCKWASHER (2) HOLZGANG #S-1004
8. 3/8" O.D.-1/4" I.D. CHROME-STEEL TUBING, 2 FEET LONG (2)
9. RUBBER CAPS (2)
10. 1/4"-20 STOVE BOLTS, 2¼" LONG (2)
11. 2½" DIAM. WOODEN DRAWER KNOBS (4)
12. 2" DIAM.-1/8" RUBBER WASHERS (2)
13. 1/4"-20 WING NUT (2)
14. 3/8" O.D.-1/4" I.D. CHROME-STEEL TUBING, 4 FEET LONG (1)
15. WOODEN BASE: 10" DIAM. x 1½", CENTER DRILLED 3/8" (1)
16. "CANDLE COVERS" (2) HOLZGANG #S-1103

A NUMBER of MONTHS AGO, THE BRITISH MAGAZINE "DESIGN" [ISSUE № 263], PUBLISHED THIS PICTURE & DESCRIBED IT AS FOLLOWS:

"ELECTRIC EEL" - LOOKING LIKE A HUGE MOUND of ILLUMINATED PASTA, THESE BOALUM LIGHTS, DESIGNED FOR ARTEMIDE MILAN BY LIVIO CASTIGLIONI & GIANFRANCO FRATTINI, CAN BE USED ON WALLS, TABLES AND FLOORS. EACH LAMP CONSISTS of A METAL & PLASTICS TUBE 180 CM. IN LENGTH [ABOUT 14 FEET] AND 6 CM. [NEARLY 2½ INCHES] IN DIAMETER, ENCLOSING A NECKLACE of 20 5-WATT BULBS."

BOTH JIM & VIC WERE DELIGHTED BY THIS "LIGHT-AS-SCULPTURE". THE PRICE, HOWEVER, IS SOMEWHAT ELITIST.

→ IF YOU OPT FOR BUILDING YOUR OWN, GO TO YOUR HARDWARE STORE & BUY ELECTRIC or GAS DRYER HOSE, IN WHITE. THIS IS PLASTIC & USUALLY 4" IN DIAMETER. THEN STRING IT WITH [LOWEST WATTAGE] CHRISTMAS-TREE LIGHTS, LIKE THE LIGHT COLUMN ON PAGE 112.
→ THIS HOSE IS SOMEWHAT EXPENSIVE. TRY FOR A SALE, WHEN YOU WILL USUALLY FIND IT IN 6-FOOT LENGTHS, & BUY TWO.

THIS IS A CHROME~
FINISHED SPOT~LIGHT
WHICH ADHERES TO
WALL~MOUNTED BASES
MAGNETICALLY.
IT IS ABOUT 5 INCHES
IN DIAMETER. THE
MOUNTING METHOD
ALLOWS IT TO BE RO~
TATED NEARLY 360
DEGREES. THUS IT
WORKS AS A SPOTLIGHT
FOR PAINTINGS or AS
A DIRECT READING LAMP
or, TWISTED AGAIN, AS
AN INDIRECT LIGHT.

▶ IT IS AVAILABLE
FROM KOVACS LIGHTS
IN N.Y., AND COMES
WITH TWO MOUNTING
CAPS. THIS MAKES IT
POSSIBLE TO LIFT THE
SPHERE OUT of ONE PLACE
& ATTACH IT ELSEWHERE.

WHITE VINYL
DISK

RING-SHAPED
MAGNET

WALL-MOUNTING
CAP,
ALUMINUM

WOOD SCREW
W/WALL
ANCHOR or
MOLLY SCREW.

FIXTURE IS FULLY
SPHERICAL TO PERMIT
SWIVEL IN ALL DIRECTIONS

SECOND, ASSEMBLED
MOUNTING CAP.

JIM'S ADAPTATION INTO AN ADJUSTABLE MAGNETIC CUBE LAMP IS ON PAGE 134.

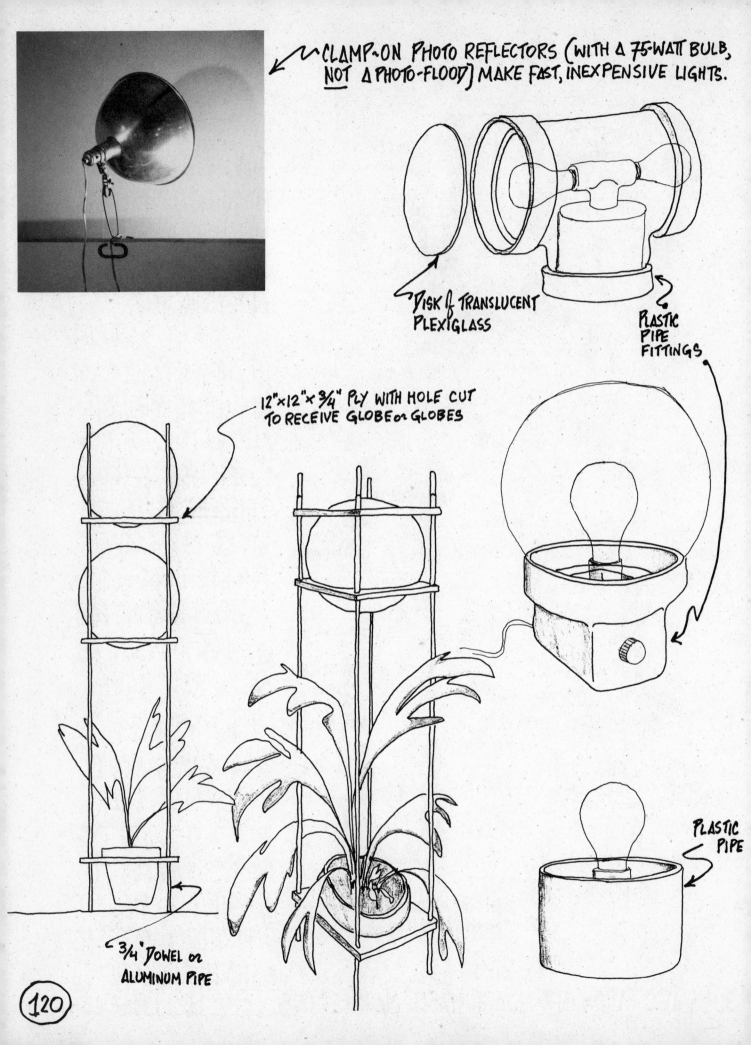

CLAMP-ON PHOTO REFLECTORS (WITH A 75-WATT BULB, NOT A PHOTO-FLOOD) MAKE FAST, INEXPENSIVE LIGHTS.

DISK OF TRANSLUCENT PLEXIGLASS

PLASTIC PIPE FITTINGS

12"×12"×3/4" PLY WITH HOLE CUT TO RECEIVE GLOBE OR GLOBES

PLASTIC PIPE

3/4" DOWEL OR ALUMINUM PIPE

# BABIES + CHILDREN:

AS MENTIONED EARLIER IN THIS BOOK, THERE ARE NO MEASUREMENTS AVAILABLE FOR SIZES, HEIGHTS, AVERAGE REACH, ETC., AS FAR AS CHILDREN [& BABIES] ARE CONCERNED.

ADMITTEDLY THIS IS SHEER LUNACY AS FAR AS HUMAN MEASUREMENT GOES, BUT HOLD ON: THERE IS ALSO NO ANTHROPOMORPHIC DATA ABOUT WOMEN, ADOLESCENTS, THE ELDERLY, OBESE PEOPLE, THE HANDICAPPED, RETURNING VETERANS WHO HAVE BEEN DISABLED, PREGNANT WOMEN OR, FOR THAT MATTER, THE 80 PERCENT OF HUMANITY LIVING ELSEWHERE THAN NORTH AMERICA, EUROPE, AUSTRALIA, NEW ZEALAND, JAPAN, RHODESIA OR SOUTH AFRICA!

WHILE BOTH VIC & JIM EXPECT TO WORK ON THIS "OVERSIGHT" BY THE DESIGN ESTABLISH~ MENT, DEVELOPING HUMAN FACTORS CHARTS FOR THIS BOOK WAS IMPOSSIBLE.

ALL THE FURNITURE FOR TODDLERS, BABIES & SMALL CHILDREN, WE HAVE SIZED ACCORDING TO OUR OWN. BOTH VIC & JIM HAVE CHILDREN OF EXACTLY THE SAME AGE, 27 MONTHS AT THE TIME OF

THIS WRITING. ALSO WE HAVE HAD ACCESS TO OTHER CHILDREN, OF COURSE.

OUR ONLY ADVICE IS: MEASURE YOUR OWN CHILD AND FREQUENTLY SEE THAT HIS OR HER FURNITURE STILL MAKES SENSE IN TERMS OF SIZES.

WE HAVE MADE NO ATTEMPT TO DESIGN ANY TOYS OR PLAYTHINGS, AS THESE TOO LIE OUTSIDE THE SCOPE OF THIS BOOK.

BUT REMEMBER THAT CHILDREN ARE NOT JUST TINY ADULTS, SOMEWHAT DIFFERENT IN SCALE. THEY HAVE GREAT NEED FOR PHYSICAL EXERCISE AND SENSORY STIMULATION THROUGH COLOURS, TEXTURES, SOUND, LIGHT, MOTION AND MUCH ELSE.

## A NOTE ON THE ELDERLY:

WHEN WE FIRST PLANNED THIS BOOK WE FELT THAT WE WOULD ALSO INCLUDE FURNITURE THAT WAS SPECIFICALLY DESIGNED FOR OLDER PEOPLE. HOWEVER, ASIDE FROM THE SPECIFICALLY DIFFERENT NEEDS OF PEOPLE IN THEIR SEVENTIES AND EIGHTIES FOR SLIGHTLY DIFFERENT RATIOS BETWEEN CHAIR-BACKS & ARM RESTS; THE MAIN NEED IS FOR HEAVY, VERY STABLE PIECES. THE ELDERLY ARE THE GROUP LEAST AFFECTED BY NOMADIC LIFE-STYLES IN OUR SOCIETY, SO THIS NOTE MUST SUFFICE.

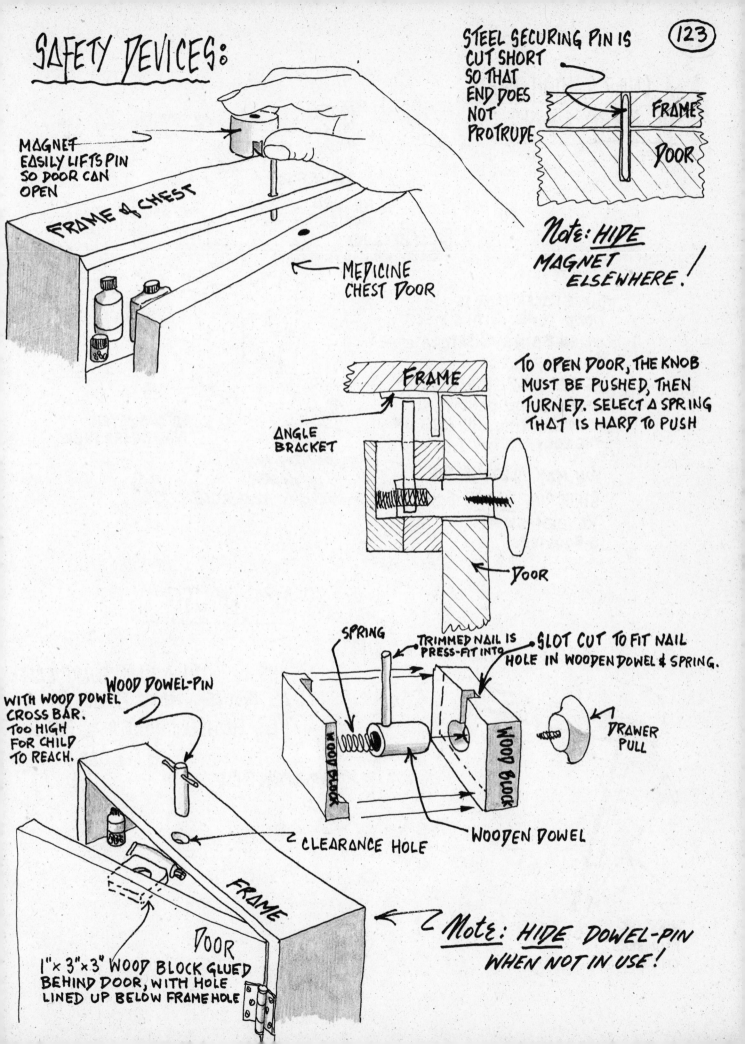

SAFETY DEVICES:

MAGNET EASILY LIFTS PIN SO DOOR CAN OPEN

FRAME OF CHEST

← MEDICINE CHEST DOOR

STEEL SECURING PIN IS CUT SHORT SO THAT END DOES NOT PROTRUDE

FRAME

DOOR

Note: HIDE MAGNET ELSEWHERE!

FRAME

ANGLE BRACKET

DOOR

TO OPEN DOOR, THE KNOB MUST BE PUSHED, THEN TURNED. SELECT A SPRING THAT IS HARD TO PUSH

SPRING

TRIMMED NAIL IS PRESS-FIT INTO

SLOT CUT TO FIT NAIL HOLE IN WOODEN DOWEL & SPRING.

WOOD BLOCK

WOOD BLOCK

DRAWER PULL

WITH WOOD DOWEL CROSS BAR. TOO HIGH FOR CHILD TO REACH.

WOOD DOWEL-PIN

CLEARANCE HOLE

WOODEN DOWEL

FRAME

DOOR

1" x 3" x 3" WOOD BLOCK GLUED BEHIND DOOR, WITH HOLE LINED UP BELOW FRAME HOLE

Note: HIDE DOWEL-PIN WHEN NOT IN USE!

# A CHILD'S HIGH~CHAIR OF FIBRE TUBING:

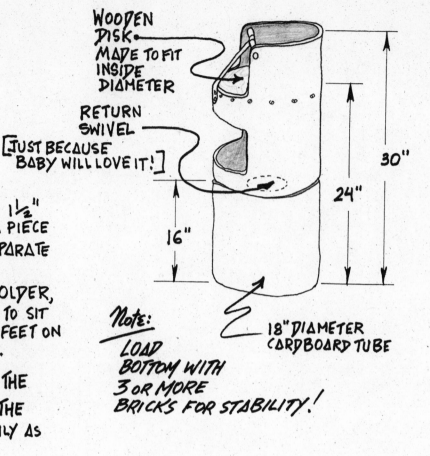

WOODEN DISK MADE TO FIT INSIDE DIAMETER

RETURN SWIVEL

[JUST BECAUSE BABY WILL LOVE IT!]

30"

24"

16"

THE SPACER BAR IS 1½" WOOD DOWEL, WITH A PIECE OF WEBBING TO SEPARATE THE CHILD'S LEGS.
AS THE CHILD GETS OLDER, HE or SHE WILL TEND TO SIT FORWARD & PUT HIS FEET ON THE LOWER CUT-OUT.

YOU MAY ALSO USE THE STRUCTURE ABOVE THE RETURN~SWIVEL ONLY AS A BOOSTER.

Note:
LOAD BOTTOM WITH 3 OR MORE BRICKS FOR STABILITY!

18" DIAMETER CARDBOARD TUBE

# ART HOUSE:

THIS IS BOTH A BLACKBOARD/EASEL AS WELL AS A MAKE-BELIEVE PLAY HOUSE. MAKE of ½" PLY or CHIP-BOARD.

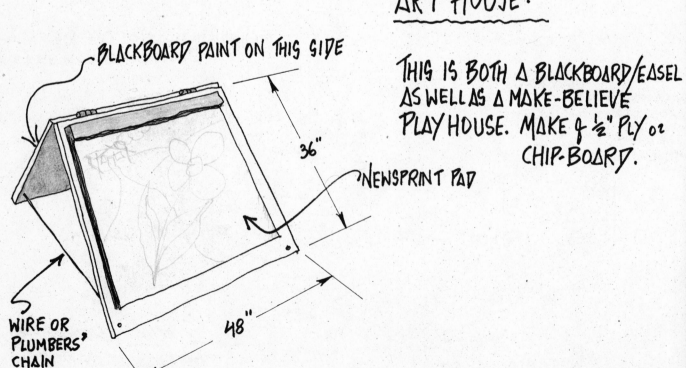

BLACKBOARD PAINT ON THIS SIDE

36"

NEWSPRINT PAD

48"

WIRE OR PLUMBERS' CHAIN

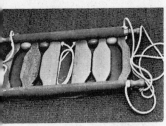

A DELIGHTFUL FOLDING,
HANGING CRADLE & A SWING.
BOTH ARE MADE of WOOD &
LINEN CANVAS. THEY WERE
DESIGNED by ANN & GORAN WÄRFF
AND ARE AVAILABLE FROM:
▶ BODA BRUKS AB,
BODA GLASBRUK, SWEDEN

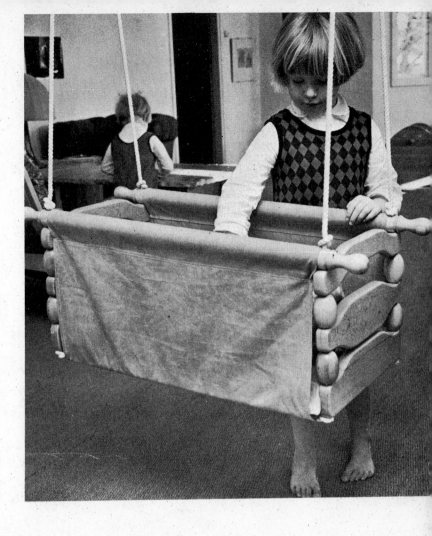

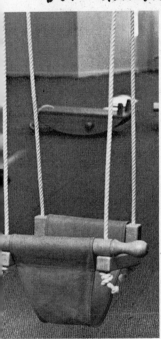

THIS STANDING CRADLE IS MADE FROM A
SECTION of A 36" DIAMETER FIBRE DRUM.

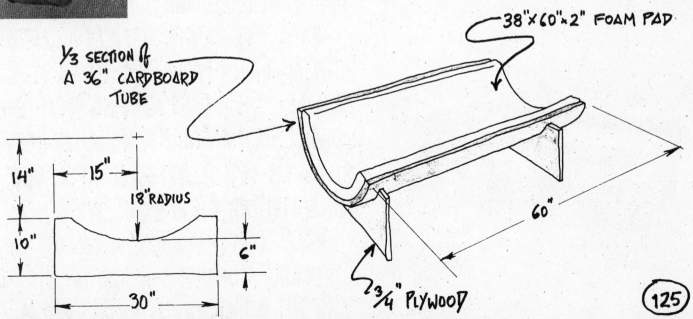

⅓ SECTION of
A 36" CARDBOARD
TUBE

38"x60"x2" FOAM PAD

14"

15"

18" RADIUS

10"

6"

30"

60"

¾" PLYWOOD

# PORTABLE BABY BED [KNOCK~DOWN]:

JIM INVENTED AND BUILT THIS BABY BED, WHICH EMPLOYS A VERY ELEGANT DOWEL-LOCKING SYSTEM. ▶ YOU MAY CHOOSE ANY DURABLE FABRIC YOU LIKE. WE USED "SWEDISH BLUE" SAILCLOTH FOR THE BOTTOM, BOTH ENDS AND THE TOPS OF THE SIDE PANELS. A VOLLEY-BALL NET WAS USED FOR THE SIDE PANELS, BUT SINCE SPORT NETS COME INSECT-PROOFED AND THEREFORE NEED CONSIDERABLE WASHING BEFORE BEING SAFE TO USE, ▶ YOU MIGHT MACRAMÉ THE SIDE PANELS INSTEAD.

▶ THE FABRIC/NETTING SHOULD BE HEMMED SO THAT IT SLIPS OVER THE WOODEN RODS EASILY. TRY TO FIT THE FABRIC AS TAUTLY AS POSSIBLE BECAUSE THIS GIVES THE INFANT ADDITIONAL SUPPORT.

▶ THE BED CAN BE USED AS A CARRIER WITH MOTHER & FATHER CARRYING IT BETWEEN THEM ON A WEBBING STRAP [NOT SHOWN]. SUCH A STRAP CAN ALSO BE USED TO TIE THE BED TO A REGULAR ADULT BED WHEN VISITING, OR TO A CAR SEAT BENCH.

▶ TO SUPPORT IT AS A BED, YOU CAN USE OUR STRUCTURE FROM OUR 3-HEIGHT TABLE [P. 56], AND PUT A 1"x2" FOAM-PAD ON BOTTOM.

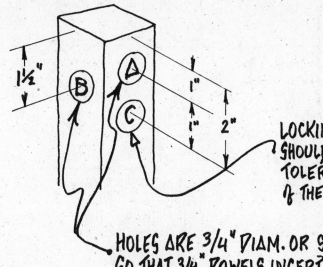

LOCKING PLUG HOLE SHOULD BE A PRESS-FIT TOLERANCE → FIT EACH OF THE 8 PLUGS SEPARATELY.

HOLES ARE 3/4" DIAM. OR SLIGHTLY LARGER SO THAT 3/4" DOWELS INSERT EASILY.

# TO CONSTRUCT THE BED:

① DRILL HOLE "A" FIRST

② INSERT 36"-LONG ROD [THERE ARE 4 36" RODS IN THE TOTAL BED] INTO HOLE "A"

③ DRILL HOLE "B" THROUGH BOTH THE 2"×2" POST [THERE ARE 4 2"×2" POSTS, EACH 12" LONG] AND THE 3/4"× 36" ROD.

④ INSERT 18"-LONG ROD [THERE ARE 4 18" RODS] INTO HOLE "B". THIS WILL LOCK THE 36" ROD.

⑤ DRILL THE HOLE FOR THE PRESS-FIT PLUG AT "C", THROUGH BOTH THE 2"×2" POST AND THE 12"×3/4" ROD. [THE 36" ROD CAN BE REMOVED FOR THIS OPERATION].

⑥ PRESS-FIT A 1½" LONG PLUG [THERE ARE 8 1½" PLUGS] INTO HOLE "C", AND THE STRUCTURE IS LOCKED.

<u>Note</u>: USE A REGULAR DRILL BIT FOR THESE OPERATIONS! A SPEEDBORE OR FLAT BIT WILL NOT WORK HERE!

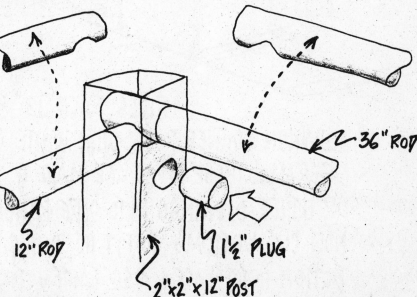

36" ROD

12" ROD

1½" PLUG

2"×2"×12" POST

▶ LEG SYSTEM TOTALLY INTERLOCKS BY RECESSING INTO EACH OTHER.

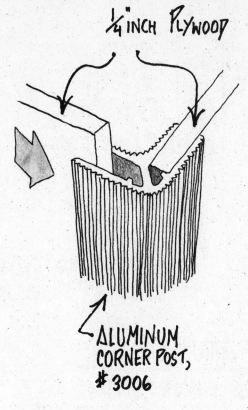

¼ INCH PLYWOOD

ALUMINUM CORNER POST, #3006

ALTHOUGH SHOWN AS A STACK, THESE PLYWOOD CUBES ARE ACTUALLY SINGLE CUBES WITH NO LINKAGES. TO MAKE A CUBE, FIRST CUT THE FOUR SIDES, EACH 18" SQUARE & INSERT IN ALUMINUM CORNER POSTS WITH WHITE "ELMER'S" GLUE, USED LIBERALLY. THESE SIDES ARE MADE OF ¼" PLYWOOD. CUT HOLES OR OTHER OPENINGS INTO SIDE PANELS BEFORE ASSEMBLY. NOW CUT BOTTOMS TO FIT IN, OUT OF ⅜" PLYWOOD. GLUE BOTTOM INTO PLACE & ALSO FASTEN TO THE SIDES WITH ¾" FINISHING NAILS. FILE & SAND EDGES OF CORNER POSTS & BOXES AND PAINT. ➜ THESE BOXES CAN ALSO BE USED FOR MOVING, OR FOR BOOK & RECORD STORAGE FOR GROWN-UPS.

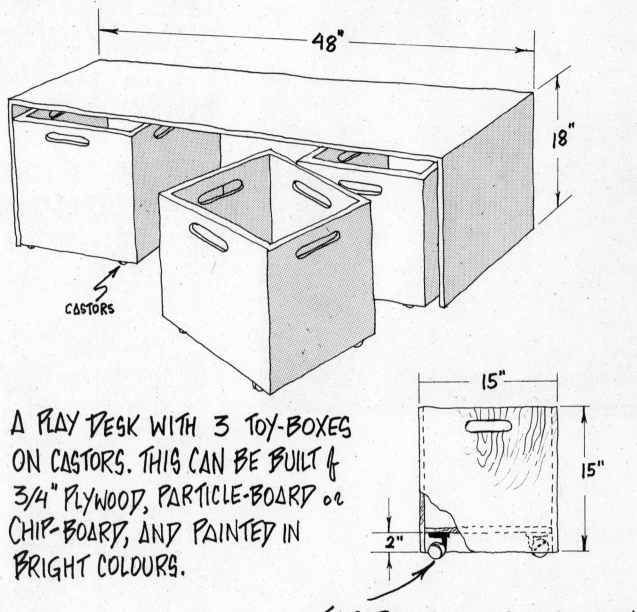

48"

18"

CASTORS

15"

15"

2"

A PLAY DESK WITH 3 TOY-BOXES ON CASTORS. THIS CAN BE BUILT OF 3/4" PLYWOOD, PARTICLE-BOARD or CHIP-BOARD, AND PAINTED IN BRIGHT COLOURS.

THIS DETAIL SHOWS ATTACHMENT OF CASTORS.

IF YOU WISH YOU CAN ALSO CUT A 15"× 15" SQUARE OF TEMPERED MASONITE & ATTACH A 12½"×12½"×2" POLYURETHANE FOAM-CUSHION TO ONE SIDE OF THE SQUARE & COVER THE CUSHION WITH FABRIC. THIS THEN "PLUGS" INTO THE BOX AS A LID OR, REVERSED, AS A SEAT. FOR MOVING THE BOXES ARE MIGHTY HANDY.

DISPOSABLE CAR SEAT:

IN ONE OF VIC'S & JIM'S CLASSES, WE FELT THAT A CAR-SAFETY SEAT FOR TOTS, MADE OF CARDBOARD, WOULD MAKE SENSE.

AMONG THE MANY STUDENT SOLUTIONS WAS THE ONE BY EDDIE COLEMAN, PICTURED TO THE LEFT.

JIM SIMPLIFIED IT SO THAT YOU CAN BUILD IT WITH NO HASSLE.

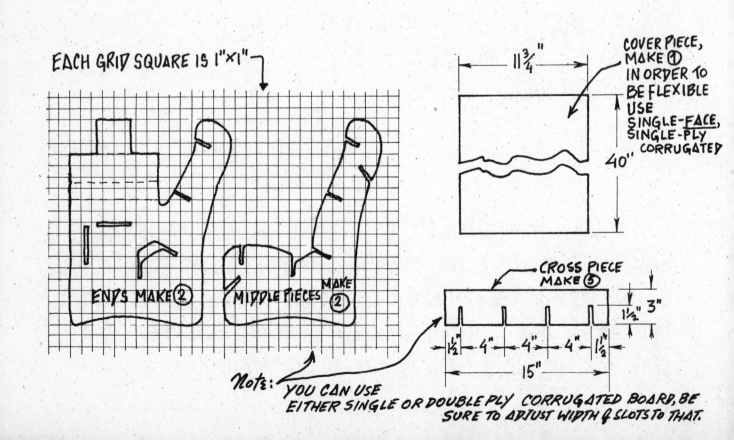

EACH GRID SQUARE IS 1"×1"

ENDS MAKE ②  MIDDLE PIECES MAKE ②

COVER PIECE, MAKE ① IN ORDER TO BE FLEXIBLE USE SINGLE-FACE, SINGLE-PLY CORRUGATED

11 3/4 "

40"

CROSS PIECE MAKE ⑤

1 1/2"  3"

1/2"  4"  4"  4"  1 1/2"

15"

Note: YOU CAN USE EITHER SINGLE OR DOUBLE PLY CORRUGATED BOARD, BE SURE TO ADJUST WIDTH & SLOTS TO THAT.

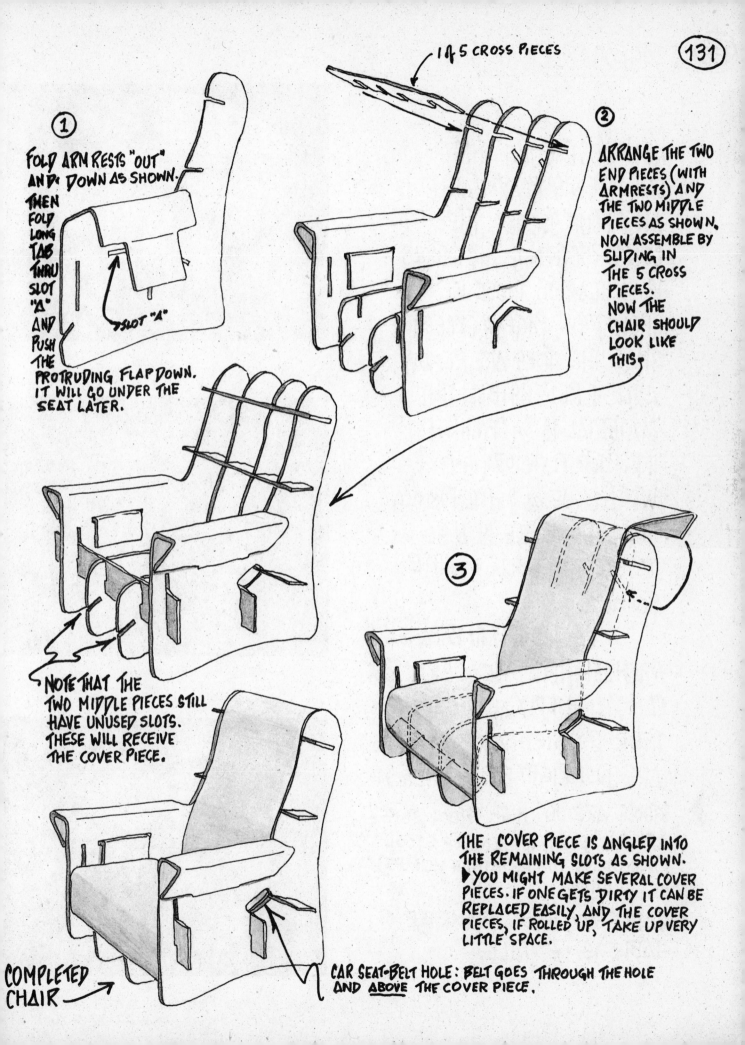

**1** FOLD ARM RESTS "OUT" AND DOWN AS SHOWN. THEN FOLD LONG TAB THRU SLOT "A" AND PUSH THE PROTRUDING FLAP DOWN. IT WILL GO UNDER THE SEAT LATER.

SLOT "A"

1 & 5 CROSS PIECES

**2** ARRANGE THE TWO END PIECES (WITH ARMRESTS) AND THE TWO MIDDLE PIECES AS SHOWN. NOW ASSEMBLE BY SLIDING IN THE 5 CROSS PIECES. NOW THE CHAIR SHOULD LOOK LIKE THIS.

NOTE THAT THE TWO MIDDLE PIECES STILL HAVE UNUSED SLOTS. THESE WILL RECEIVE THE COVER PIECE.

**3**

THE COVER PIECE IS ANGLED INTO THE REMAINING SLOTS AS SHOWN.
▶ YOU MIGHT MAKE SEVERAL COVER PIECES. IF ONE GETS DIRTY IT CAN BE REPLACED EASILY, AND THE COVER PIECES, IF ROLLED UP, TAKE UP VERY LITTLE SPACE.

COMPLETED CHAIR

CAR SEAT-BELT HOLE: BELT GOES THROUGH THE HOLE AND ABOVE THE COVER PIECE.

KEN YOST BUILT THIS
CHILDREN'S PLAY-TABLE
AND FOUR STOOLS. THE
CONSTRUCTION OF THE STOOLS
IS SIMILAR TO THOSE WE
SHOWED ON PAGE 44, EXCEPT
THAT THE TOPS ARE REMOV-
ABLE & REVERSIBLE. THE
MATERIAL IS ¾" FINNISH
IMPORTED PLYWOOD [14-PLY],
WITH BLUE OR WHITE FORMICA
TOPS. THE TABLE IS ALSO
COVERED WITH BLUE & WHITE
FORMICA.

AS JENNI SATU PAPANEK,
MICHAEL HENNESSEY & ERIK YOST
CAN DELIGHTEDLY AFFIRM AFTER
THEIR 2ND BIRTHDAY PARTY, SIZES
ARE JUST RIGHT FOR TODDLERS:

▶ STOOLS ARE 10" HIGH, STOOL TOPS
ARE 9½" DIAMETER; ENTIRE STOOL
(INCLUDING TOP RETAINER HUMPS)
IS 11" WIDE.
TABLE-TOP IS 36" DIAMETER &
TABLE IS 17" TALL.

# etc:

IT IS REALLY VERY SATISFYING TO ACTUALLY, HAPPILY HANDWRITE A BOOK LIKE THIS. THE WRITING ITSELF BECOMES DISTILLED, UNTIL IT IS BOTH LUCID AND PERSONAL, LIKE WRITING A LETTER.

NOW THE BOOK IS DONE. WE ARE BOTH AWARE OF HOW MUCH WE HAD TO LEAVE OUT [AS TOO COMPLEX TO SELF~BUILD, TOO COSTLY, MUCH TOO PERSONAL, ETC.]. DIMLY WE ARE ALSO AWARE OF HOW MUCH ELSE WE HAVE LEFT OUT, WITHOUT MEANING TO.

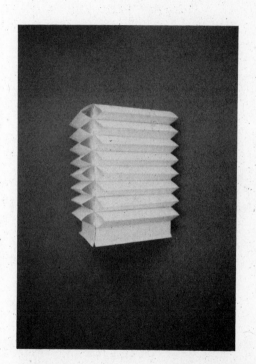

BUT THEN, THIS IS THE FIRST BOOK OF ITS KIND. THE REASON FOR NOT GIVING YOU A BIBLIOGRAPHY IS SIMPLE: NO OTHER BOOKS ON HIGHLY PORTABLE FURNITURE [WITH OR WITHOUT A DO-IT-YOURSELF SLANT], EXIST. IF YOU WANT TO READ MORE: WAIT A WHILE! THIS BOOK WILL START SIMILAR WORK BY OTHERS.

ON THESE LAST FOUR PAGES WE HAVE SOME THINGS WE FELT SHOULDN'T BE LEFT OUT. THE PICTURES HERE ONLY HINT THAT YOU CAN INTELLIGENTLY FOLD PAPER OR PLASTIC TO GIVE IT STRENGTH & BODY FOR A LAMP.

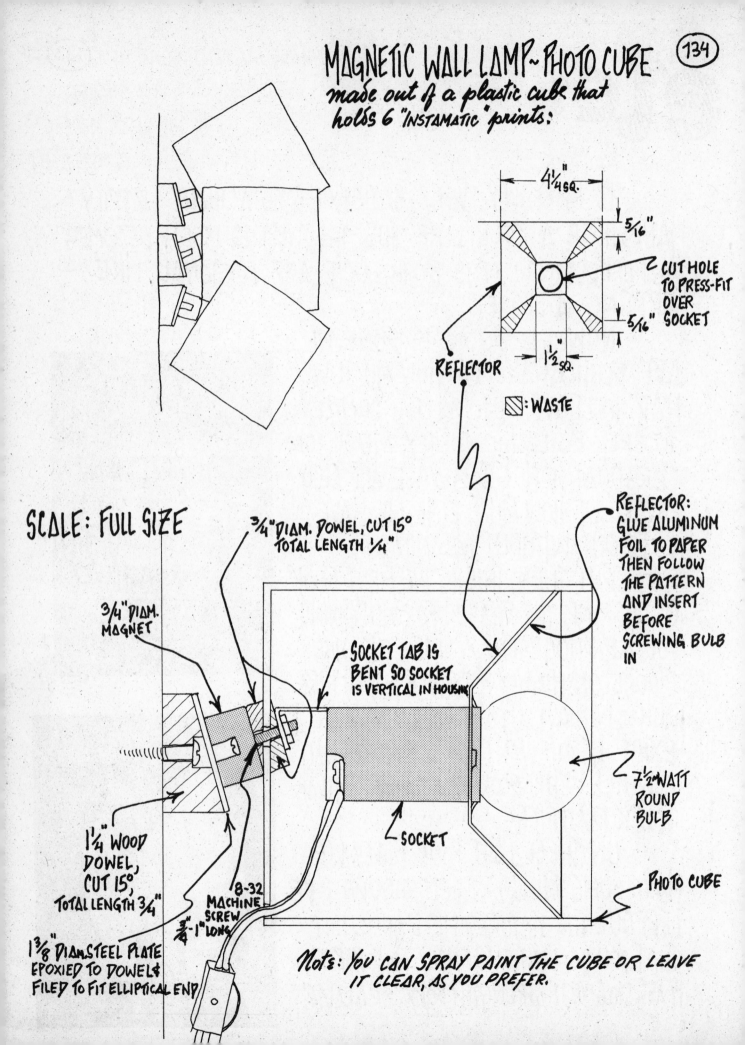

# MAGNETIC WALL LAMP ~ PHOTO CUBE
*made out of a plastic cube that holds 6 "Instamatic" prints:*

4¼" SQ.

5/16"

5/16"

1½" SQ.

CUT HOLE TO PRESS-FIT OVER SOCKET

REFLECTOR

▨ : WASTE

SCALE: FULL SIZE

¾" DIAM. DOWEL, CUT 15°, TOTAL LENGTH ¼"

¾" DIAM. MAGNET

SOCKET TAB IS BENT SO SOCKET IS VERTICAL IN HOUSING

REFLECTOR: GLUE ALUMINUM FOIL TO PAPER THEN FOLLOW THE PATTERN AND INSERT BEFORE SCREWING BULB IN

7½ WATT ROUND BULB

SOCKET

PHOTO CUBE

1¼" WOOD DOWEL, CUT 15°, TOTAL LENGTH ¾"

8-32 MACHINE SCREW ¾"-1" LONG

1⅜" DIAM STEEL PLATE EPOXIED TO DOWEL & FILED TO FIT ELLIPTICAL END

*Note: YOU CAN SPRAY PAINT THE CUBE OR LEAVE IT CLEAR, AS YOU PREFER.*

# SPEAKER SYSTEM:

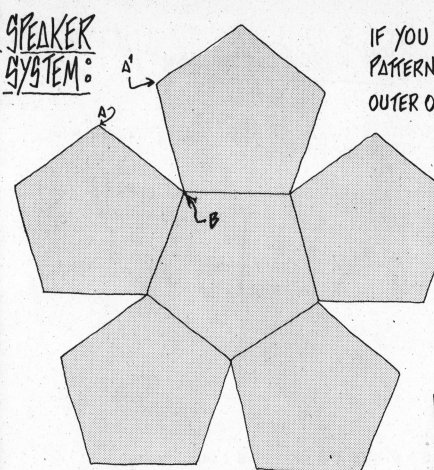

IF YOU HAVE SIX PENTAGONS IN THIS PATTERN, AND BEND THE FIVE, SHADED, OUTER ONES <u>UP</u>, UNTIL THE SIDES MEET [EXAMPLE: SIDE A-B MEETS SIDE A¹-B], YOU HAVE BUILT <u>HALF</u> OF A GEOMETRIC SOLID CALLED A DODECAHEDRON. [IT HAS 12 FACES, ALL PENTAGONS]. THEN ASSEMBLE BOTH HALVES.

VIC DISCOVERED SOME TIME AGO THAT IF YOU EXTEND THE EDGES OF A DODECA~ HEDRON <u>OUTWARD</u> IN A REGULAR MANNER [SEE PHOTO BELOW], THEN THE ANGLES OF EACH OF THESE TWELVE FIVE~SIDED HORNS COINCIDE NEARLY EXACTLY WITH OPTIMUM SOUND DISPERSION ANGLES.

WITH THIS KNOWLEDGE FOR STARTERS, DOUGLAS SCHOEFFLER BUILT 2 DODECAHEDRAL SPEAKERS OUT OF FIBREGLASSED CARDBOARD. WE PURPOSEFULLY USED THE LEAST EXPENSIVE, TINNY SPEAKERS WE COULD GET AT 73¢ EACH. THE 24 SPEAKERS, MOUNTED AS SHOWN, GIVE SUPERB $400.- SPEAKER SOUND EXCEPT FOR BASS REFLEX. ▶ WE WON'T SHOW YOU HOW TO BUILD THIS; EXPERI- MENT YOURSELF. FOR PENTAGONS, TURN.

# How to Draw a Pentagon:

**1** USE COMPASS TO DRAW A CIRCLE. THE PENTAGON WILL FALL WITHIN THE DIAMETER.

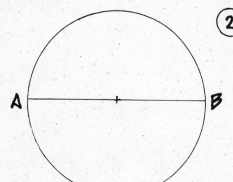

**2** DRAW THE DIAMETER HORIZONTALLY THROUGH THE CENTER: A-B

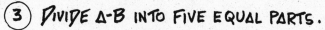

**3** DIVIDE A-B INTO FIVE EQUAL PARTS.

**4** SET THE COMPASS TO THE LENGTH of A-B. SCRIBE TWO ARCS, ONE FROM "A" & ONE FROM "B" TILL THEY INTERSECT ABOVE THE CIRCLE.
NOW DRAW A LINE FROM THIS INTERSECTION THROUGH THE <u>SECOND</u> DIVISION AND TO THE OPPOSITE RIM of CIRCLE: POINT "C".

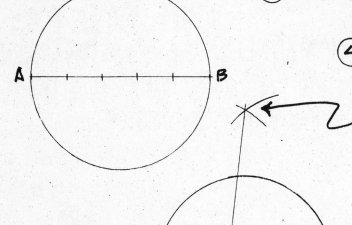

**5**

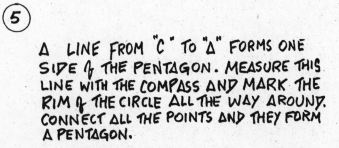

A LINE FROM "C" TO "A" FORMS ONE SIDE of THE PENTAGON. MEASURE THIS LINE WITH THE COMPASS AND MARK THE RIM of THE CIRCLE ALL THE WAY AROUND. CONNECT ALL THE POINTS AND THEY FORM A PENTAGON.

# HINTS FOR WORKING:

- WRITING A STEP~BY~STEP DESCRIPTION ON HOW TO BUILD EVEN THE SIMPLEST FURNITURE PIECE IS SILLY. MOREOVER IT WOULD BE A GARGANTUAN TASK, FRUSTRATING TO US AND CONFUSING TO THE READER.

- THE PURPOSE BEHIND THIS SECTION IS TO OUTLINE THOSE THINGS YOU'LL NEED TO BUILD THE FURNITURE IN THIS BOOK.

▶ TOOLS: A LOT COULD BE SAID ABOUT VARIOUS TYPES, BRAND~NAMES & USES, BUT YOU CAN BUILD THE FUR~ NITURE WE'VE SHOWN WITH THESE:

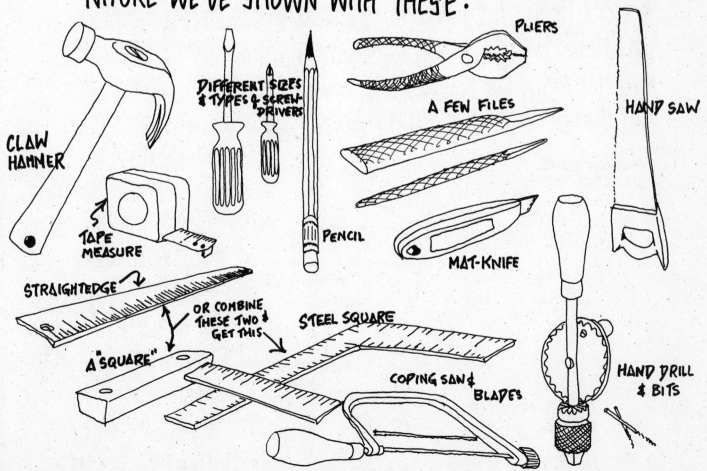

PLIERS

DIFFERENT SIZES & TYPES & SCREW~ DRIVERS

A FEW FILES

HAND SAW

CLAW HAMMER

TAPE MEASURE

PENCIL

MAT~KNIFE

STRAIGHTEDGE

A "SQUARE"

OR COMBINE THESE TWO & GET THIS

STEEL SQUARE

COPING SAW & BLADES

HAND DRILL & BITS

• IF YOU HAVE ACCESS TO POWER~TOOLS, AN ELECTRIC DRILL IS USEFUL. BIG PANELS CAN BE CUT WITH A CIRCULAR SAW; A SABRE SAW WORKS FOR GENERAL~PURPOSE CUTTING OR MAKING SLOTS. REMEMBER: SOPHISTICATED TOOLS IN THE HANDS OF A GOOD CRAFTS~ MAN GIVE BETTER RESULTS: A DRILL~PRESS CAN MAKE A CLEANER, STRAIGHTER HOLE THAN YOU COULD BY HAND. CONVERSELY, FINE DETAILS CAN OFTEN BE ACHIEVED BY CAREFUL HAND WORK.

• CRAFTSMANSHIP IS KNOWING WHICH TO USE WHEN. IT'S EASY TO GET ALL INVOLVED WITH POWER~TOOLS — SO WHEN IN DOUBT, GO CAREFULLY BY HAND — IT'S SLOWER BUT YOU ARE IN CHARGE.

• IF YOU NEED POWER~TOOLS, BORROW OR RENT THEM. BE CONCERNED ENOUGH ECOLOGICALLY TO NOT ADD TO POLLUTION & WASTEMAKING BY BUYING WHAT YOU MAY USE RARELY.

▶ DRILL BITS:   A CONVENTIONAL DRILL BIT IS EXCELLENT FOR GENERAL~PURPOSE WORK, SOFT METALS, WOOD AND EVEN PLASTICS. [SPECIAL DRILLS FOR PLASTICS ARE NOW ON THE MARKET.] THE SPEEDBORE BIT IS FOR WOOD ONLY, BUT IT IS SUPERB FOR MOST WORK. IT DRILLS EASILY, MAKES A CLEAN HOLE & WON'T SPLINTER THE WOOD.

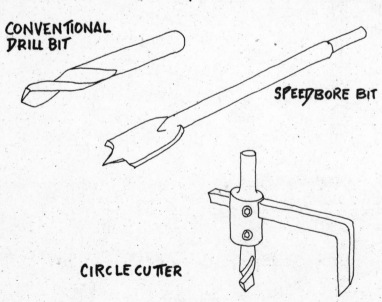

CONVENTIONAL DRILL BIT

SPEEDBORE BIT

CIRCLE CUTTER

▶ FOR VERY LARGE HOLES [1½" OR MORE], USE A CIRCLE CUTTER. SINCE THERE ARE MANY DIFFERENT ONES ON THE MARKET, THEY MAY DIFFER FROM THE SKETCH.

CIRCLE CUTTERS MUST BE USED WITH EXTREME CAUTION AND ONLY ON A DRILL-PRESS. [THEY WORK VERY WELL ON PLASTICS TOO!]

# WOOD

HERE IS A CHART SHOWING THE VARIETY OF SIZES YOUR LOCAL LUMBER DEALER SHOULD HAVE IN STOCK:

| LINEAR LUMBER | | SHEET LUMBER* | |
|---|---|---|---|
| ASK FOR: | TRUE SIZE: | ¼" PLYWOOD | 4'×4', 4'×8' |
| 1"×2" | ¾"×1½" | ½" PLYWOOD | AS ABOVE |
| 1"×3" | ¾"×2½" | ¾" PLYWOOD | AS ABOVE |
| 1"×4" | ¾"×3½" | *CHIP-BOARD & MASONITE COME IN THE SAME SIZES. ▶ PLYWOOD CUT-OFFS CAN OFTEN BE BOUGHT CHEAPLY! | |
| 1"×6" | ¾"×5½" | | |
| 1"×8" | ¾"×7¼" | | |
| 1"×10" | ¾"×9¼" | 36" DOWEL RODS, DIAMETERS: | |
| 1"×12" | ¾"×11¼" | ⅛" | ¾" [ALSO IN 8-10-12 FT. LENGTHS AS MOLDING] |
| 2"×2" | 1½"×1½" | ¼" | ⅞" |
| 2"×4" | 1½"×3½" | ⅜" | 1¼" |
| 2"×6" | 1½"×5½" | ½" | 1" AS WELL AS 1½" & 2" |
| 4"×4" | 3½"×3½" | ⅝" | COME ALSO IN 8,10 & 12 FOOT LENGTHS [SEE ¾" ABOVE] |

WHEN BUYING LINEAR LUMBER, ALWAYS HAND-SELECT THE WOOD FOR CLEANLINESS & STRAIGHTNESS. SIGHT DOWN THE LENGTH TO SPOT BOWS OR WARPS. LOOK FOR KNOT-HOLES, LOOSE PLUGS or SPLITS. ONCE YOU'VE BOUGHT IT, IT'S YOUR PROBLEM, SO BE FINICKY!

▶ <u>CORRUGATED CARDBOARD:</u>

SINGLE PLY

SINGLE PLY IS USED IN MOST OF OUR CORRUGATED FURNITURE WHERE EASE OF AVAILABILITY, EASE OF CONSTRUCTION AND COST ARE IMPORTANT.

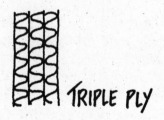

DOUBLE PLY

DOUBLE PLY IS USED IN FURNITURE THAT MUST SUPPORT A GREAT DEAL OF WEIGHT, SUCH AS CHAIRS & BEDS.

TRIPLE PLY

TRIPLE PLY HAS NOT BEEN USED IN THIS BOOK → IT IS RIDICULOUSLY EXPENSIVE AND HARD TO FIND.

SINGLE PLY-
SINGLE FACE

SINGLE PLY - SINGLE FACE [AS WE CALL IT] IS HIGHLY BENDABLE & THEREFORE USED AS COVER OR CONTOUR.

▶ <u>TO CUT CORRUGATED USE A MAT-KNIFE.</u> THE CONVENTIONAL UTILITY KNIFE & AN "X-ACTO" KNIFE ARE SHOWN. REPLACE BLADES OFTEN TO INSURE SHARPNESS. ALWAYS GUIDE THE KNIFE WITH A <u>STEEL</u> STRAIGHTEDGE, TO GET CRISP EDGES & CLEAN LINES.

## STRENGTH:

▶ ALWAYS POSITION THE CORRUGATED SO THAT THE "S" LAMINATIONS ARE VERTICAL.
AS THE ILLUSTRATION SHOWS, CARDBOARD DERIVES ALL ITS STRENGTH FROM THIS KIND OF ALIGNMENT.
BE CAREFUL TO ALWAYS USE CARDBOARD IN THIS WAY IN ALL FURNITURE THAT YOU BUILD.

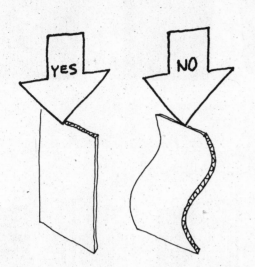

## ACCESS:

▶ YOU CAN ALWAYS GO TO A PAPER MANUFACTURER AND FIND SHEETS OF CORRUGATED. SINGLE AND DOUBLE PLY COME IN ALMOST ANY SIZE, EVEN IF YOU NEED ENORMOUS SHEETS.
SINGLE PLY ~ SINGLE FACE COMES IN HUGE ROLLS, ABOUT 4 FEET HIGH AND 6 FEET IN DIAMETER.
THE BEST AND MOST AVAILABLE SOURCE IS THE LOCAL APPLIANCE STORE. ONE REFRIGERATOR CARTON WILL BUILD ALMOST ANYTHING IN THIS BOOK.

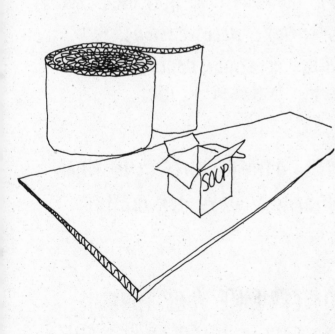

AN INGENIOUS "INVISIBLE"
CYLINDER HINGE.

FOR 180° OPENINGS &
MADE OF PROFILE BRASS.

▶ FROM: SISO EXPORT LTD.
26 NYROPGGADE
1602 COPENHAGEN
DENMARK

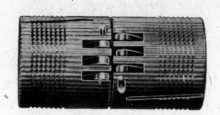

FOR ALL OF THE FURNITURE THAT USES CASTORS,
WE'VE SPECIFIED "BALL"-CASTORS.
THE LARGEST SELECTION EASILY AVAILABLE
IS MADE BY ▶ BASSICK, INC.

USE "ELMER'S" OR OTHER WHITE GLUE WHEN
GLUING WOOD AND ALWAYS USE CLAMPS.

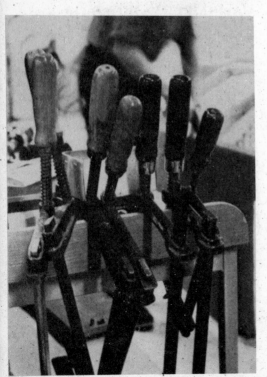

ON ANY PROJECT: TAKE YOUR TIME; IF
YOU RUN INTO DIFFICULTIES → GET THE
HELP OF SOMEONE EXPERIENCED.
Good Luck!

Lamp

dimensions approx

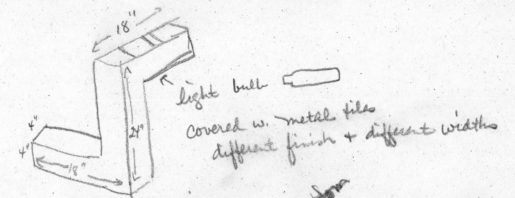

light bulb

covered w. metal tiles
different finish + different widths

uprights + side bottom piece

Chair

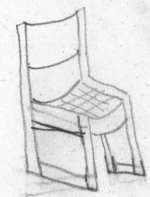

uprights 1'4" square solid wood
front + back approx 1 x 3 or 4 *
back w definite curve, front w slight
   curve
seat covered w woven 1" strips of
   natural leather
back solid piece 8" wide
                        $60 $70

* reinforced only at to corners
plugs at all holes – darker color

NOTES & CALCULATIONS:

# NOTES & CALCULATIONS:

(146) NOTES & CALCULATIONS: _____

# NOTES & CALCULATIONS:

NOTES & CALCULATIONS:

PHOTOGRAPHIC CREDITS:

WE WISH TO THANK THE MANUFACTURERS, PERIODICAL PUBLISHERS & PHOTOGRAPHERS WHOSE MATERIAL APPEARS IN THIS BOOK. HERE ARE OUR SOURCES:

BACK COVER PHOTOGRAPH BY RICHARD HOUGH

P. 73: LENNARD, COURTESY: "MOBILIA" MAGAZINE, DENMARK

P. 88, 89: LOUIS SCHNAKENBURG, "MOBILIA"

P. 36: COURTESY: "MOBILIA", ALSO P. 142

P. 76: TIM STREET-PORTER, COURTESY: "DESIGN", GREAT BRITAIN

P. 39: KUVAAMO LUOMA, HÄMEENLINNA, FINLAND

P. 26: ADVERTISEMENT FOR DUX MÖBLER & SWEDEN, COURTESY: "&/SDO" MAGAZINE, HELSINKI, FINLAND

P. 20, 21: JIM & PENNY HULL, LOS ANGELES

P. 37: COURTESY: "ARCHITECTURAL DESIGN", ENGLAND

P. 107: ADVERTISEMENT © by "INNERSPACE", 1972

P. 115: KAIJA AARIKKA, FINLAND

P. 85, 98, 108, 118 & 125: ARE FROM MANUFACTURER'S ADVERTISEMENTS IN ITALY, GERMANY, SWEDEN & THE U.S.

P. 22, 23 & 46: PAT FAURE, LOS ANGELES

P. 15, 34, 38, 40, 44, 52, 55, 62, 64, 102, 111, 112, 116, 117, 119 & 130: PETER KARNIG

ALL OTHER PHOTOGRAPHS ARE BY JIM HENNESSEY & VICTOR PAPANEK.

VICTOR PAPANEK    JAMES HENNESSEY